# SHAKESPEARE'S MELANCHOLICS

# SHAKESPEARE'S MELANCHOLICS

by

## W. I. D. SCOTT

*With a foreword by Henry Yellowlees,*
O.B.E., M.D., F.R.F.P.S.

**MILLS & BOON LIMITED**
50 GRAFTON WAY, FITZROY SQUARE
LONDON, W.1

REF

PR

2989

.S35

1962

PRINTED IN GREAT BRITAIN
BY EBENEZER BAYLIS AND SON, LTD.
THE TRINITY PRESS, WORCESTER, AND LONDON

# CONTENTS

# ACKNOWLEDGEMENTS

FOREMOST, I wish to thank Dr Henry Yellowlees, not only for his kind contribution of a foreword, but primarily for teaching me that Shakespeare and Psychology are synonymous.

My thanks are also due to the members of Chester Theatre Club, and to Dorian Williams, director of the Pendley Shakespeare festivals, for providing me with my experience of Shakespearian acting and production.

The Librarian of Cheshire County Students Library has been particularly helpful in obtaining for me copies of the various works necessary for my study.

For permission to quote I am indebted to the following:

Princeton University Press, publishers of *The Organization and Personnel of the Shakespearean Company*, by T. W. Baldwin.

Collins, publishers of *Shakespeare*, by Ivor Brown.

Rupert Hart-Davies, publishers of *The First Night of Twelfth Night*, by Leslie Hotson.

Routledge and Kegan Paul, publishers of *Psychological Types* and *Modern Man in Search of a Soul*, by C. G. Jung.

Methuen & Co., publishers of *The Crown of Life* and *The Sovereign Flower*, by G. Wilson Knight, and of *Shakespeare's Sources*, by Kenneth Muir.

Oxford University Press Inc., publishers of *The Question of Hamlet*, by Harry Levin.

Clarendon Press, Oxford, publishers of *Character and Society in Shakespeare*, by Arthur Sewell.

Longmans, Green & Co., publishers of *Character and Motive in Shakespeare*, by J. I. M. Stewart.

Chatto & Windus, publishers of *The Shakespearean Ethic*, by John Vyvyan.

and to Professor George Watson, for permission to quote from his broadcast lecture entitled *Three Ways to Shakespeare*.

Other works to which I have made passing reference are listed in the Bibliography.

Finally, I wish to record my thanks to Mrs Joan Bryant, of Mills & Boon, for many valuable suggestions and emendations, and for compilation of the Index.

# FOREWORD

DR SCOTT has paid me the compliment of inviting me to contribute a foreword to this book.

Apart from my personal friendship and regard, my only qualification for doing so is that I made a very small contribution towards his medical education at St Thomas's Hospital, and found him more than usually responsive to the Shakespearian references and quotations, with which I used to embellish my lectures. I find it hard to believe that those lectures played even the smallest part in helping to arouse the interest and enthusiasm which are so obvious throughout this able and scholarly work.

I feel that the title of the book does much less than justice to the nature and scope of its contents, in spite of Dr Scott's fascinating exposition of the meaning of the word "Melancholy" in Elizabethan times, in Chapter 1. The following chapter has nothing directly to do with Shakespeare at all, but was certainly necessary if the subsequent ones are to be understood. It is nothing less than a synopsis of modern medical psychology for lay people, and I find it of particular personal interest, because for many years the task of "educating the public" in psychiatric matters has been one of my greatest interests, and, indeed, preoccupations. It may well be that something less comprehensive might have sufficed, because this chapter could stand very creditably by itself as a summary for medical students, but its comprehensive nature, broad but never shallow, is in keeping with all the later chapters.

These are far more than clinical descriptions of the characters named, few, indeed, of whom would be called melancholics or depressives nowadays, under any modern classification. Each chapter is an intensive study of the character from the psychological point of view, and in relation to the plot of the play, the other characters in it, the views of critics and psychologists from the Elizabethan age to the present day, and what they have inferred or believed about Shakespeare's own mind and purposes.

The late Sir Arthur Quiller-Couch said that he was content simply to wonder at the miracle of Shakespeare, and to leave to the critics the task of explaining him. It certainly can be argued that the more profound and technical criticism becomes, the more apt is the music and beauty of words to elude it. Nevertheless, those who are not satisfied merely to wonder at Shakespeare's poetry, and leave it at that, have here an excellent chance of studying the lines along which modern psychological criticism goes, and the peculiar merit of this book is that after such study the reader will find his wonder not diminished but increased.

HENRY YELLOWLEES.

# AUTHOR'S INTRODUCTION

AN addition to the spate of Shakespearian criticism calls for the justification at least of a new approach or a different kind of critic. But this requirement may be modified by the kind of reader the critic hopes to attract.

For nearly three centuries after his death the published criticism of Shakespeare's plays was from professional writers of poetry and prose, many of them little less eminent than Shakespeare himself—such as Ben Jonson, Dryden, Samuel Johnson, Pope and Coleridge. Since the advent of A. C. Bradley, at the end of the nineteenth century, the Professors of Literature have held the field almost unchallenged, with only occasional skirmishes from poets and psycho-analysts, and—rarest of all—from actors and other men and women of the Theatre; although many of the critics have combined a professional approach to the language of the plays with practical experience of amateur acting or production.

Studies of the morbid psychology inherent in the plays have been made by professional psychiatrists and by interested literary critics whose knowledge of psychological medicine is only theoretical. Similarly the psychiatrists have usually shown a limited interest in the literary and dramatic qualities of the plays.

In my case the professional approach is that of a doctor familiar with the theory and practice of psychological medicine, but with an experience of mankind drawn mainly from the intimate problems encountered in the ordinary routine of general medical practice. My approach as an amateur is equally practical: during the past fifteen years I have been fortunate enough to have been involved, as producer or actor, in the amateur presentation of a large number of Shakespeare's plays, and it is from the need for interpreting on the stage a wide selection of his characters that my interest in their melancholy has been drawn.

Whilst I hold no claim to literary scholarship, I have made every effort to familiarize myself with the writings of others better informed and instructed. In this way I have tried to avoid mere repetition of views which have been formed by those approaching the same subject by a different route, and to give proper consideration to opinions which are in opposition to mine.

Professor George Watson, in a recent broadcast lecture (August 1960), summarized the recent history of Shakespearian criticism as follows:

1. Character analysis held the stage until 1914, whereby critics such as Bradley analysed the characters as if the plays were psychological novels.
2. There followed a German and American School, fiercely historical and practical, disallowing all considerations of character outside the play itself, and dealing mainly with theatrical convention.
3. During the last three decades, an Anglo-American School, founded by Professor Wilson Knight, has studied the plays as if they were poems, concerned with spacial analysis and total significance, indifferent to their dramatic qualities.

Professor Watson reminds us that Shakespeare's plays are not novels, historical documents nor poems, but plays, and considers that a new school of criticism should concern itself with their dramatic form and structure, akin to that which Dryden and Johnson tried to establish, but more constructive in character. He admits that the ultimate significances are there, and that a study of the language may help to reveal them, but he denies the possibility of a return to the school associated with Bradley.

Of necessity, my own criticism is mainly concerned with the presumably extinct character analysis. But a main part of my thesis is that in the plays of Shakespeare the characters govern the plot and the structure, and I have tried to pay a good deal of attention to the precise way in which they do this.

To Aristotle, plot was more important than character;

thought, language and song came lower down in the scale, and spectacle was considered to be outside the author's province, wherein lies a possible condonation of the exuberance of some modern producers of Shakespeare. The great Greek tragedies transcend Shakespeare in all but character—their themes, although more primitive, deal more closely with the roots of morality—but their heroes are removed from ordinary mortal level, symbolic of something larger than themselves, and nearer to gods than to the individuals and types we know and meet in ordinary life.

Shakespeare wrote his plays with particular characters in mind, which he was incapable of falsifying to meet the exigencies of plot or dramatic construction, and I hope to show that it is this faithfulness to observed truth which is responsible for certain of the developments in his plots at variance with his original sources which have aroused most speculation among his critics.

Professor J. I. M. Stewart considers that the classical line of Shakespearian criticism is from Dr Johnson through Coleridge and Bradley to Freud. Possibly the first three of these can be allowed to pass into history, but criticism on psycho-analytical lines must go further than Freud. The simpler psychology of Alfred Adler has been unconsciously inherent in many of the views of critics of all periods, but only John Vyvyan has paid more than cursory attention to the most lately deceased, and perhaps greatest of the triumvirate, Carl Jung. As in the case of Adler, a good deal of Jung's psychology is embodied in some modern criticism, particularly the recognition of what Jung first postulated directly, the existence of racial memories in the unconscious layer of the mind. Wilson Knight gives expression to this idea as follows: "In Shakespeare a common racial store of impressions, rooted deep in antiquity, echo from the fringes of consciousness their ancient significances". I leave detailed consideration of psycho-analytical theory to a later chapter, but I am surprised that no Shakespearian criticism has yet appeared paying tribute to Jung's great work on *Psychological Types*. The recognition of the basic attitudes of introversion and extraversion seems to me particularly important for understanding both Shakespeare's characters themselves and his own relationship to them, to which much of recent criticism has been devoted.

Following a plan that I found useful when trying to interest my medical colleagues in the subject of Hamlet's melancholy, my approach to each of the characters I have chosen follows the lines of a clinical consultation, using evidence from the text of the play as it proceeds, but also from my own study both of Elizabethan and modern psychology. Psychological theories change, but psychopathic patients have always been the same. We may no longer accept Elizabethan and Jacobean theories of the causation and treatment of mental disorder, but the clinical picture is one as true today as it was 350 years ago.

By speculating about the past history of Shakespeare's characters and ascribing to them motives outside the text I fall foul of Professor Arthur Sewell, who states that artistic damage is done to a play by adducing what is not given by the playwright. S. L. Bethell extends a warmer welcome to the intending critic—in his opinion that "a dramatist may express meanings of which he is himself only dimly aware, and his methods may be dictated by an end which he is not consciously seeking; the real reason for his doing this or that can be discerned only when the work is finished and understood". At the same time Mr Bethell warns us not to go too far. He considers that the reason why Shakespeare does not always reveal the mental processes whereby his characters form a wrong or sinful judgement may be because, like Hamlet, he regards the depths of human personality as inviolable, and objects to those who would "pluck out the heart of my mystery".

It is true that in a novel, and sometimes in a play, a more powerful effect can be achieved by leaving certain things to the imagination. Henry James, in *The Turn of the Screw*, conjures up an atmosphere of horror enhanced by the lack of any reference to the exact nature of the evil power held over the children by the dead valet and maid. But in the representation on the stage—*The Innocents*—I experienced this as a defect. When one could actually view the ghosts and observe the reaction of the children to them it was demanding too much of the imagination to leave unexplained the details of the life in the household prior to the arrival of the new governess.

Some plays, like some jokes, can certainly be spoilt by explanation. When Eddie Cantor, applying for a job, says to his prospective employer: "I can take care of the children, and if there aren't any children I can take care of that", we understand precisely what he means, and explanation can only make a witty joke vulgar. But when James says to Hancock: "The trouble with you is that you are like everyone else—you hate you", there is a wealth of philosophy behind the remark, which could be expanded to fill a volume. And so with Shakespeare the compression of character within the lines is such that many additional motives may be inferred without departing in spirit from the text. This compression becomes more evident to anyone undertaking the formidable task of making cuts in one of his longer plays for public performance.

T. S. Eliot, also, deplores the critic who uses his frustrated creative talent to write creatively about Shakespeare's characters instead of studying the plays as a whole, but I hope to show that it is possible to do both.

I have chosen my eight examples of the melancholic character for a variety of reasons, but mainly because of my own special interest in them. There are many others which I could have included, but the particular eight—all absolutely distinct from each other—make up a fairly comprehensive representation of the various types of melancholy known both to Elizabethan and to modern psychology, all delineated by Shakespeare with startling accuracy of observation.

It was the opinion of Pope, quoted by G. B. Harrison, that: "Every single character in Shakespeare is as much an Individual as those in life itself; it is impossible to find any two alike". Dr Johnson carries this opinion further: "Shakespeare is above all other writers, at least above all modern writers, the poet of nature; the poet that holds up to his readers a faithful mirror of manners and of life. His characters are not modified by the customs of particular places, unpractised by the rest of the world, by the peculiarities of studies or professions, which can operate but on small numbers; or by the accidents of transient fashions or temporary opinions. They are the genuine progeny of common humanity, such as the world will always supply, and observation will always find. His persons act and speak by the influence of those general passions and principles by which all minds are agitated, and the whole system of life is continued in motion. In the writings of other poets a character is often an individual; in those of Shakespeare it is commonly a species."

In approaching my characters as if I were making a professional diagnosis I am comforted by the view of Professor Wilson Knight that criticism of them should not be from an ethical standpoint. But in general the literary critics are determined to keep professional psychology in its place—in the world of science, not of art. Professor Sewell says that psychology is the handmaid, not the mistress, and that moral responsibility takes over at the important point of decision; but that is not the common experience in life, which Shakespeare is so concerned to mirror truthfully.

There is a general unwillingness among literary critics to accept mental disorder as a valid motivating force in Shakespeare's characters. Obsessed with the idea that drama must record and discuss moral issues, they miss the limitation which Shakespeare himself put upon his purpose, as expressed by many of his characters when functioning as it were without the play as a commentating chorus. Othello's final lines explicitly repudiate a moral judgement:

> "Speak of me as I am; nothing extenuate
> Nor set down aught in malice."

Less often quoted, but equally apposite, is the commentary of the Poet, introducing *Timon of Athens*:

> I have in this rough work shaped out a man
> Whom this beneath world doth embrace and hug
> With amplest entertainment. My free drift
> Halts not particularly, but moves itself
> In a wide sea of wax. No levelled malice
> Infects one comma in the course I hold;
> But flies like an eagle's flight, bold forth and on,
> Leaving no tract behind.

In other words, Shakespeare's characters are what they are, and because of what they are the events are shaped; they are not the less, but even more, fit subjects for tragedy because a mind in normal health would have succeeded where they fail.

Bradley in particular is emphatic in his insistence on moral issues. He says that "Shakespeare occasionally, for reasons which need not be discussed here, represents abnormal conditions of mind—insanity, somnambulism, hallucinations, and deeds arising from these are not deeds expressive of character. Lady Macbeth's sleepwalking was not the cause of anything; Macbeth did not murder Duncan because he saw a dagger in the air; Lear's insanity and Ophelia's were the result not the cause of the conflict. If Hamlet were really mad at any time he would cease to be a tragic character."

Although I disagree with the concluding premise, there is, of course, sound judgement in this appraisal of the limited examples which Bradley has chosen. But why need Shakespeare's reasons "not be discussed here"? This seems an ingenuous attempt to avoid a discussion that might lead to the wrong conclusion.

Even a critic well versed in modern psychological theory can be guilty of the same kind of evasion. Writing of Antonio, L. A. G. Strong says that "there is a temptation to examine his state of mind from the angle of his behaviour to Shylock, but I am afraid it must be resisted." Why must it be resisted? Surely not because it would prove an uninteresting digression, but perhaps because it might let some unpleasant cat out of the bag, as I hope to show in a later chapter.

This resistance to deep psychological exploration attains a peak of absurdity in Harry Levin's: "Even professional alienists have offered their diagnosis of Hamlet's insanity". Surely the professional psychiatrist (the term in normal use in Great Britain) is the only person who can ratiocinate sensibly on insanity, whether found in literature or in real life. The trouble is that the critics have not kept themselves informed of modern views on insanity. Bradley indeed cannot be fairly blamed for opinions which were those natural to his period, but we are now living in an era of enlightenment on mental disease at least as far ahead of the turn of the century as Shakespeare's time was of the Middle Ages.

Polonius may say: "To define true madness, what is't but to be nothing else but mad?", but he was not exactly presented to us by Shakespeare as a character whose opinions are infallible. There is no sharp division of behaviour into either the rational, based on valid moral considerations, or the irrational, implying certifiable irresponsibility; the distinction is only operative at rare extremes. Character and motivation are largely irrational and non-moral in all of us, however much we may persuade ourselves to the contrary. It is true that there are well-defined mental illnesses from which only a few of us will suffer, although not many escape depression in some modified form. But even so, only a minority of those afflicted can be described as "nothing else but mad". For the most part, the impact of their irrationality on the events in which they are concerned is a fit subject for such absorbing interest as is evident in Shakespeare's plays. If in his approach to his characters he allowed his free drift to move itself "in a wide sea of wax", surely his critics may do the same.

It is certainly my intention to approach his melancholics without bias of any kind, to examine them through the words he has put into their own mouths and into those of their companions, and then to consider the effect of their mental peculiarities upon the plot and structure of the play in which they appear. Coleridge says that "the characters in Shakespeare are to be inferred by the reader; they are not told to him. He must build up a picture from what his friends say, his enemies say, and some chorus-like person such as the Fool says", and it is my intention to conduct my examination of them upon these lines.

I hope that among the readers of this book there will be both members of my own profession who have an interest in, rather than a profound knowledge of, the plays of Shakespeare, and general readers who are concerned with him as a dramatist rather than as a poet. With this end in view I have quoted more extensively from the text than is usual in a work of criticism, to avoid the need for constant cross-reference by those who are not completely familiar with the play in question; and I have also included a chapter summarizing the main conceptions of medical psychology, as understood by the general practitioner rather than the specialist in mental diseases.

I have endeavoured to prepare for this book by extending as widely as possible my reading of existing Shakespearian criticism germane to my subject. In so vast a bibliography it is inevitable that I shall have missed many works that I should have studied, but to study all would be in itself the work of a lifetime.

At this point I should like to make it clear that whilst I deprecate the restriction of Shakespearian criticism to university departments of English Literature, it is to their professors that I must express myself particularly indebted for a foundation of scholarship without which no such criticism as mine—partly more and partly less specialized—could be attempted. This kind of scholarship I cannot emulate; in the words of A. C. Bradley himself, I can only hope to "present something of that close familiarity with the plays, that native strength and justice of perception and that habit of reading with an open mind" which make "many an unscholarly lover of Shakespeare a far better critic than many a Shakespearian scholar".

# 1

# MELANCHOLY IN SHAKESPEARE'S TIME

It is fortunate that we have available today Robert Burton's comprehensive treatise: *The Anatomy of Melancholy*. Published in 1621, this work could not have been read by Shakespeare, but the subject matter is that familiar to men of learning in his time. There is an earlier work on Melancholy, by Dr Timothy Bright, published in 1586, from which Professors Kenneth Muir and Dover Wilson have quoted with reference to Hamlet, and which I propose to introduce into my chapter on that character. The modern authority on melancholy in Elizabethan times is Lawrence Babb, whose work: *The Elizabethan Malady, a Study of Melancholy in English Literature from 1580–1640* has provided me with much material.

Although he does not confine himself to depressive states as we understand them today, and his basic psychopathological theory is now exploded, Robert Burton attacks his subject in a concise and scientific manner, classifying melancholy according to its causation and manifestations, then proceeding from symptoms and signs to differential diagnosis, prognosis and treatment with the clarity of a good modern textbook.

The following is a graphic description of classical melancholia, as true today as it was 300 years ago:

"Although they be commonly lean, hirsute, uncheerful in countenance, withered and not so pleasant to behold, by reason of those continued fears, griefs and vexations, dull, heavy, lazy, restless, unapt to go about any business: yet their memories are most part good, they have happy wits and excellent apprehensions. . . . Fear and sorrow are no common symptoms to all melancholy. I find some that are not so at all. Some indeed are sad and not fearful; some fearful and not sad; some neither fearful nor sad; some both".

19

In this passage Burton is noting the variable combinations of depression and anxiety which are a commonplace of observation today. He goes on:

"Some (are) afraid they are damned or shall be. They are troubled with scruples of conscience, distrusting God's mercies, think they shall go certainly to Hell, the Devil will have him, and make great lamentation. . . . A third (type) fears all old women as witches . . . every person comes near him is maleficiated, every creature, all intend to hurt him and seek his ruin. . . . Yet for all this (their morbid fears) . . . in all other things they are wise, staid, discreet, do nothing unbecoming their dignity, person or place, this foolish, ridiculous and childish fear excepted. . . . Sorrow is that other character, without evident cause, grieving still, but why they cannot tell: never laughing, sad, thoughtful. . . . Suspicion and jealousy are general symptoms: they are commonly distrustful . . . testy, petty, peevish. There is nothing so vain, absurd, ridiculous, extravagant, impossible, incredible, so monstrous a chimaera, so prodigious and strange, such as Painters and Poets durst not attempt, which they will not readily fear, feign, suspect and imagine unto themselves."

Burton then introduces the prevailing astrological conceptions. They behave according to their guiding star: "If Venus they are still courting of their mistresses, most apt to love, amorously giddy. . . . They seem to hear music, plays, see fine pictures, dancers, merriment and the like". Those born under Saturn are very melancholy; under Jupiter ambitious and with delusions of grandeur; under Mars "choleric, rash and furious"; under Mercury "solitary, contemplative, subtle—Poets and Philosophers"; under the moon "restless and all for travel—sea voyages—delighting in water, fishing, etc.".

For an understanding of all psychological theory of Shakespeare's time the basic postulate of bodily "humours" must be considered. There are four humours, which were described as sanguine, choleric, phlegmatic and melancholic, according to the predominant fluid in the body. The seat of the blood was thought to be the liver, of the bile the gall-bladder, of the phlegm the lungs or kidneys and of the black melancholic fluid the spleen.

Dr Timothy Bright appears to be the authority on humours, quoted both by Lawrence Babb and Burton:

"The sanguine man is fleshy, ruddy, fair-haired, amiable of countenance and manner, gladsome of spirits, kindly, liberal, fond of good food and good wine, fond of music, amorous, intelligent, courageous. The choleric person is lean, hairy, saffron-coloured, rash, quick to anger, proud, revengeful, ambitious, shrewd. The phlegmatic man is short and fat, pale, torpid, slothful, mentally dull. . . . Melancholy men are lean, dry, lank . . . the face beneath pale, yellowish, swarthy. . . . As touching the notes and marks of their minds they are churlish, whining, obstinate, greedy. . . . They use a certain slow pace and soft nice gait, holding down their heads, the countenance and look grim and frowning. They are taciturn, they love to be alone, and they are continually tormented by fears and sorrows."

The types of melancholy associated with the different humours are described by Bright as follows:

"Phlegmatic melancholy causes pallor, headache and much weeping, delighting in waters and ponds and fishing. Sanguine melancholy, with ruddy complexion, causes laughter, wit and merriness . . . much given to music and dancing and to be in women's company. Sometimes their laughter is immoderate and uncontrollable." Choleric melancholy causes quarrelsomeness and violence—"they sleep little and in their fits you shall hear them speak all manner of languages—Hebrew, Greek and Latin, that were never taught or knew them before. . . . Choleric melancholy makes men able to endure death and all manner of torments with invincible courage. . . . Saturnine melancholy causes sadness and solitariness—fear—suspicion, dreams of graves and death and think themselves dead." If the humours are mixed the symptoms are mixed.

Melancholy is further subdivided by Burton into head melancholy, windy hypochondriacal melancholy and melancholy of the whole body. He remarks that Aristotle has long since maintained that melancholy men may be witty, and that learned men such as lawyers and philosophers are inclined to be melancholy. Aristotle says that there is no excellent wit without a mixture of madness.

Burton is almost as prodigal in his theories of the general causation of melancholy as are modern psycho-analysts; immediate causes he lists as fear, sorrow, suspicion, studying and "horing". He anticipates Freud by considering that both too much and too little "venery" may play a part.

In a separate discussion of love melancholy Burton instances
heroic love as causing melancholy by enervating the bravest
soldiers and most generous spirits, but rates it bad only when
immoderate and mutable. Jealousy he classes as a deformed
branch of love melancholy, taking as an example Henry IV's
jealousy of Richard II and then of his own son, Henry V—
another foretaste of Freud. The stars and climate may cause
jealousy, also idleness and impotence. "If an ugly or deformed
man marry a beautiful woman he is apt to be jealous"—an
opinion plainly applicable to Othello and according with the
modern theory of Adler. The symptoms of jealousy given by
Burton are those of the condition which we recognize today
by the name of paranoia.

Burton's prognosis of melancholy in general can be summarized as follows:

Physical signs such as skin eruptions, purging and much
urination indicate a good prognosis; he evidently appreciates
that the organic psychoses are more likely to be acute and temporary. "It is less dangerous if imagination only and not reason
be affected" (i.e. a neurosis rather than a psychosis). It is more
chronic in women. Suicide is common, and the form it takes is
often dramatic. In this connection Burton introduces a note of
modern enlightenment: "We should not judge the melancholic
suicides, but trust God to be merciful to them." Prognosis of
the jealous type is bad: "proceeding from suspicion to hatred,
frenzy, madness, injury, murder and despair", which is much
our own experience with cases of paranoia.

Burton's recommended treatments can be only briefly enu-
merated:

1. By God and prayer.
2. Physic is of little help, and one should beware of greedy
   doctors: "Many of them, to get a fee, will give Physic
   to every one that comes, when there is no cause", an
   accusation to which, in modified form, the medical profession of today is no stranger.
3. The patient must be willing to be cured, and have some
   hope that his physician can help him.
4. "Physic itself in the last place is to be considered."
5. Diet, of various kinds.

6. Appeasement of the sexual appetite.
7. Change of climate. The Cotswolds and Sutton Coldfield are mentioned as particularly beneficial.
8. Change of scene.
9. Exercise of body and mind.
10. Rectification of sleep and dreams by habit, posture, etc.
11. Confession of grief to a friend, and good company.
12. Humouring of fantasies. Burton quotes the delightful example of a man who was "afraid to piss lest the town be drowned"; the suggestion that it was on fire and needed the water was productive of immediate relief.
13. Music, except obsessive compositions to a loved one.
14. The best remedy for love melancholy is a suitable marriage.
15. The prophylaxis of jealousy is similarly by prudent matches. It may be relieved by occupation and company.

Burton recognizes a separate entity of religious melancholy. He considers the causation to be from the Devil, heretics, simplicity, blind zeal, ignorance, solitariness and pride. Symptoms include fanaticism, obstinacy and peevishness. The prognosis is bad: "They cause wars and disruption, finishing with suicide." If gentle persuasion fails to cure them there is no alternative to the deprival of their liberty. Modern history can provide many such examples.

Lawrence Babb quotes freely from Burton and from Bright, on whose works his description of Elizabethan psychopathology is based.

He finds a particular inclination to melancholy in the writers of the period. This, he considers, appeared in Italy at the time of the Renaissance, largely due to the popularity of Aristotle at that time. According to Babb, Aristotle considered that most great writers were of a melancholy disposition, and Burton himself says that he wrote of melancholy to be busy—to avoid melancholy. Babb says that, in *L'Allegro* and *Il Penseroso*, Milton rejects violent melancholy but welcomes scholarly melancholy of the Aristotelian type. He draws attention to the setting of many of Shakespeare's plays in Italy and to the Italian, or vaguely foreign, nationality of the melancholy characters.

Babb describes a primary malcontent type, with a sense of

neglected superiority, deepened by disappointment and frustration; he cites Armado in *Love's Labour's Lost* as an example of this. Other types are the melancholic villain, the melancholic cynic and the melancholic scholar, the latter possibly inclusive of the melancholy writers. I will consider these categories of melancholy in more detail in the chapters devoted to the individuals of my series.

It is evident that to the Elizabethans melancholy comprehended a wide range of mental attitudes, from a normal and praiseworthy gravity of bearing, through mild eccentricity, to established neurosis and the wildest psychotic derangement. For comparison with modern conceptions reference is required to practically the whole of psychiatry, which is indeed embraced by the sum of Shakespeare's characters themselves.

In my next chapter I attempt a survey of the basis of psychological medicine today.

# 2

# MODERN MEDICAL PSYCHOLOGY

To FORM a basis for understanding references to present-day psychology, with its somewhat formidable technical jargon, I must now give a summary of the essential framework.

Abnormal mental states have long been divided into what are called "Psychoses" and "Neuroses". The criteria for this distinction are as follows:

1. ORIGIN. Heredity is a more important factor in the psychoses and environment in the neuroses.
2. SYMPTOMS. A psychotic is less likely to know that he is ill, and that the trouble lies in his mind. Delusions and hallucinations only occur in the psychoses.
3. PROGNOSIS. There is a tendency for psychotics to deteriorate and become demented; they more commonly commit suicide. Neurotics retain their reason, even when incurable.
4. TREATMENT. Physical methods are only appropriate to the psychoses, and analytical methods to the neuroses. Drug treatment is common to both.

In practice, many sufferers from melancholia, a disease classified with the psychoses, know perfectly well that they are mentally ill; whereas many hysterics and hypochondriacs, classed as neurotic, resist strongly any suggestion that their symptoms are of mental origin. But severe melancholics, as in other psychoses, suffer from a defect in reason which may be such as to make them unaware of their need for treatment. Neurotics are more likely to suffer from emotional defects, which may be accompanied by obsessions, but which are accessible to rational explanation. The distinction between a delusion and an obsession is important. A delusion may be defined as a belief in something which would be incredible to another person of the same age, sex, race, social class and religious creed, this belief persisting in spite of all proof to the contrary. All these factors may be found in an obsession, except the last, which is the vital distinction.

The commonest psychosis—melancholia—is seldom referred to by that name nowadays, and, as I have observed, many depressive states impinge upon the borderland between true psychoses and neuroses. As a great deal of reference will be made to depression in ensuing chapters, I must attempt a brief classification of the common varieties:

## A. PRIMARY DEPRESSION
1. Endogenous, or arising without ascertainable cause—including:
2. The manic-depressive psychosis, comprising attacks of depression alternating with periods of elation and variable spells of normality between. The depressed phases are usually more marked than the elated, which may amount to no more than a period of exceptional well-being.
3. Involutional depression, occurring during the period of degenerative glandular changes in men and women in their forties and fifties. A history of precedent depression is commonly absent, and the attack generally lasts longer than the recurrent type.
4. Reactive depression, dependent on a known and recognizable cause, such as bereavement or other emotional shock.

## B. SECONDARY DEPRESSION
This may occur in the course of another psychosis, or as a sequel to some physical disturbance such as influenza or childbirth.

I now list other common psychoses:

## C. SCHIZOPHRENIA
Contrary to popular belief this does not produce a dual personality, but a splitting of the functions of the mind which normally work in harmony: thought, feeling and action, or in psychological language: cognition, affect and conation. In schizophrenia, although bizarre delusions and hallucinations are notable features, they result, not from a primary defect of reason, but from an inability of

the functions of the mind to operate as a unit. If thought and reason are most affected, with prominent delusions, we speak of the paranoid form of schizophrenia; if emotional expression is the most abnormal we call this the hebephrenic type—if action, the catatonic. This last term arises from the peculiar tone of the muscles of the body, whereby there may be either abrupt attacks of impulsive violence or a remarkable immobility known as "flexibilitas cerea", or waxy flexibility, causing the subject to adopt the posture of a waxwork.

## D. PARANOIA

This psychosis frequently manifests itself at first merely as an awkward obstinate temperament, with the insidious development of definite delusions—commonly of persecution or of infidelity in the marriage partner. An almost reasonable basis for the delusions is often developed in remarkable detail, but it is an axiom that the false belief is maintained in spite of all proof to the contrary, and logical reasoning with the patient is useless. There is so little deterioration in the mentality apart from the fixed delusions that the patient can often lead a comparatively normal life; but there is at present no known curative treatment.

## E. PARAPHRENIA

This is a milder form of delusional insanity, commoner in females. It causes vague delusions and hallucinations without systematization; the subjects are often regarded merely as mildly eccentric.

## F. ORGANIC PSYCHOSES

In the types mentioned above no organic change has ever been found in the brain, although it is possible that this has been so far missed. In the organic group there is some infection or toxic process responsible for the symptoms. In the acute variety the state is usually one of confusion and disorientation; recovery is the rule when the organic condition has subsided. The classical chronic form is the psychosis due to syphilis of the brain, known as general paralysis of the insane, or dementia paralytica. Delusions of grandeur are the significant feature, with ideas of omnipotence or boundless wealth. The subjects are usually friendly and cheerful, but the delusions may be of a melancholy type. Fortunately, with modern prophylaxis and early treatment, this psychosis is becoming relatively uncommon. In the fully developed stage it can be ameliorated but never cured by treatment.

## G. PSYCHOPATHIC PERSONALITY

This is the name given to an ill-defined mental state causing persistent antisocial conduct, but without the characteristic pattern of schizophrenia or other distinct psychosis. The basic defect appears to be in the capacity for experiencing concern for the well-being of others. Unable to love, the subjects can only hate, and cannot conform to the pattern of behaviour required by society. It is difficult to find legal justification for keeping them under restraint in a mental hospital, and many spend most of their lives in prison.

In attempting a similar sketch of the neuroses I am on more debatable ground. Even today, "neurasthenia" or "nervous debility" are terms commonly used by doctors to avoid a more precise classification. Freud coined a neat system of diagnostic labels—comprising conversion hysteria, anxiety hysteria, anxiety neurosis, obsessional neurosis and neurasthenia; he also made a distinction between true neurosis and psychoneurosis. But however attractive in theory, this exact differentiation has not stood the test of time.

Personally, I find it convenient to adopt a simpler division of the neuroses into motivated and unmotivated types, which really correspond to extraverted and introverted reactions. Motivated neuroses include hysteria and hypochondria, whereas anxiety and obsessional states fall into the unmotivated category. It must be emphasized that hysteria in the psychological sense does not mean violent weeping and wringing of the hands, but a subjective conviction that there is something wrong with some part of the body, which is not borne out by objective fact. The hysteric, characteristically, does not react emotionally to the symptoms, exhibiting what is termed a "belle indifférence". Hysteria and hypochondria occur in people of constitutionally inadequate personality, who have never faced up squarely to the normal problems and difficulties of life, unconsciously making use of their symptoms to avoid what is unpleasant or to gain positive ends. They tend to cherish their symptoms, and the suffering from them devolves mainly on their relatives and friends.

Anxiety and obsessional states occur more frequently in people reasonably well adjusted to the normal problems of life, under the stress of some exceptionally difficult situation, often over which they have no personal control. Their suffering may be intense, and they often conceal their symptoms out of a sense of shame. Pathological anxiety is an excess of apprehension in circumstances which would cause some distress to a normal person. The symptoms arise without any immediate external cause, though often in predictable circumstances, as in confined spaces—a phenomenon known as claustrophobia. In an anxiety state the symptoms are felt emotionally rather than perceived intellectually. Obsessional states arise from similar causes, but dominate the intellectual sphere, causing obsessive thoughts and compulsions to irrational action—usually harmless to others though disturbing the general life of the individual.

I regard the distinction between these two main groups of neuroses as important, because, whereas the motivated neurotics have an inherent resistance to effective treatment, much can be achieved with the unmotivated by an understanding approach, even though the basic situation may be unalterable.

Whilst the categories of mental abnormality may be quite easily defined, given some agreement on the terminology to be used, psychological theory has always been mutable, showing regular swings between mechanistic and metaphysical points of view. Prior to the second half of the nineteenth century unscientific speculation on astrological and demonological lines had prevailed over a long period. In the revolt which followed the spread of scientific knowledge over all branches of medicine an attempt was made to ascribe all mental disease to specific organic changes in the brain, even if these could not be directly demonstrated. The pendulum swung back again with the equally extreme search of the followers of Freud for repressed material in the unconscious mind to account for psychotic as well as neurotic illness. But whilst psycho-analysis has proved a disappointment in practice, it has led, mainly through the influence of Alfred Adler, to a valuable reassessment of psychological factors in what used to be considered entirely organic diseases—such as asthma, peptic ulcer and hyperthyroidism.

During the past few decades there have existed in London two largely dissenting schools: the Maudsley Hospital and The Tavistock Clinic. The Maudsley Hospital has maintained a strict regard for a scientific approach, based on the precepts of clinical medicine and morbid pathology; whereas the Tavistock Clinic has propagated the more speculative views of the psycho-analytical school. Recently the academic psychologists have obtained a foothold in psychiatry, with a return to something like the mechanistic approach of the late nineteenth century. Professor Eysenck, of the Maudsley Hospital, whose work has attained some prominence both in this country and the United States, scolds his psychiatric colleagues for their lack of accurate method in diagnosis and controlled research in treatment. He and his followers have built up a vast system of statistical analysis intended to correlate causation, symptoms, signs, treatment and prognosis on a more scientific basis.

It will be apparent that my sympathies and interest lie more with the psycho-analytical school, but this does not mean that I regard the opposite view as erroneous. Both approaches have their contribution to offer. The conflict, as in the whole of life, it between basic psychological types, which are as relevant to the psychiatrist as to his patients. It is inevitable that a lover of Shakespeare, whether introverted or extraverted, should tend more towards the intuitive and feeling personalities than to the thinking and sensation of the pure scientist. Nevertheless, a respect for scientific method has led me to minimize the effect of unconscious conflicts in the minds both of Hamlet and Timon, which I do not consider appropriate to the diagnosis I have made; and in general I have as much concern for the psychological atmosphere of the plays as a whole—reflective of the mind of the author—as for the individual analysis of the character under review.

There is no doubt that Freud's discovery of the unconscious mind was the most important advance in psychology that has ever been made. All modern medical psychological theory is dependent on this conception, and the language of psycho-analysis is now so much the commonplace of everyday life that those who abuse Freud most roundly can only do so in the terms of which he himself was the originator.

Freud visualizes a mind which has unconscious, preconscious and conscious levels. Impulses from the unconscious level reach the preconscious in dreams, and influence consciousness when awake, characteristically in lapses of speech and memory. When an unconscious impulse exerts a violent and persistent influence on thought or behaviour Freud refers to it as a COMPLEX.

He divides the total personality into three parts. The most primitive, existing only at the unconscious level, he calls the ID. Overlying the whole is the SUPER-EGO or EGO-IDEAL. This is the kind of person the individual would like to be, and the super-ego also acts as a critic at the unconscious level. The central figure, the EGO, derives its existence from the id below it and the super-ego above it; it is partly conscious and partly unconscious.

Freud describes the driving force of the personality as the LIBIDO. This does not mean physical lust, though he regards it as sexual in the broadest of senses. In infancy the libido is directed towards the self—the so-called narcissistic phase. In early childhood it becomes transferred to the mother, and later to individuals of the same sex. The transference to the opposite sex should take place during adolescence. This natural sequence is important, because Freud holds that both psychoses and neuroses, and also abnormal sexual behaviour in adult life, are caused by failure of the normal transference to take place—by fixation at one of the stages, or by a reversion to an earlier phase, which he calls REGRESSION.

If an impulse of the libido is resisted because the super-ego disapproves of it, Freud uses the term REPRESSION; but it must be emphasized that this repression is done unconsciously by the individual himself. The popular equation of repression with the more familiar conscious suppression is erroneous. But it is not necessary for the super-ego to repress a disagreeable impulse; it may instead be diverted to less primitive and socially more useful channels. For instance, a man with a superabundance of sexual energy may devote some of it to artistic expression in music or painting. This process is known as SUBLIMATION.

The second of the triumvirate, Alfred Adler, accepts the Freudian premise of the different levels of the mind, but considers that the sexual libido is less important than what he calls the WILL TO POWER, of which an amusing variant is the one-upmanship of Stephen Potter. This desire to be important is a natural and useful motivating force in its right proportion. If it is thwarted by some physical or other disability, a sense of inferiority develops, of which the individual is unaware, and which Adler describes as an INFERIORITY COMPLEX. Like the repression of Freud this complex is always unconscious, and the common ascription of any form of timid behaviour to an inferiority complex is usually groundless. If the feeling of inferiority is due to some physical defect or peculiarity Adler uses the term ORGAN INFERIORITY. The unnatural aggression which often cloaks this complex he defines as OVERCOMPENSATION.

The psychological theories of Carl Jung are more complicated and more comprehensive than those of the preceding pair. Jung, in the course of his long, active life, has made use of material drawn from all races at all times. His psychology is not only a study of the personality past and present, but a dynamic synthesis directed also to the future. Whereas Freud's method of analysis is purely redactive Jung's is prospective. Freud claimed to do no more than reveal what was hidden—he had nothing to add, whereas it was Jung's aim to use the material revealed for a positive new integration of the personality.

Apart from the wider range of his approach to the problems of the individual, Jung's chief contribution to psychological theory is, perhaps, his conception of the COLLECTIVE or racial UNCONSCIOUS. Whereas Freud comprehended only a storehouse of memories and impulses from foetal life onwards, Jung adds to this a separate compartment for instinctive phenomena derived from the history of the race, operating parallel with the personal unconscious. He accepts Freud's libido and Adler's will to power as natural motives but postulates a spiritual force, acting in opposition to both of these. He is thus able to include ethnology, mythology and comparative theology in his scheme.

Jung's structure of the personality, as given by Iolande Jacobi, is somewhat different from Freud's. In place of the id, the ego and the super-ego he describes a basic personality, partly conscious, partly unconscious, which he calls the EGO, with a wholly conscious superimposition: the PERSONA, corresponding partly to Freud's ego-ideal, but implying an actual outward personality as shown to the world rather than an ideal personality which is aimed at. He regards the persona as something necessary and complementary to the ego, and equally in need of a satisfactory stability.

Roughly corresponding to Freud's id is Jung's SHADOW, an ambivalent element in the unconscious, which has both helpful and noxious components. Jung also describes an unconscious contrasexual figure, the ANIMA or ANIMUS, representing a balancing or complementary ideal of the opposite sex, which he regards as important in marriage and in later life. Embracing the whole personality are two archetypal figures, the GREAT MOTHER and the WISE OLD MAN, which Jung regards as relevant to the integration of the total psyche.

Jung's second great contribution to psychological theory is his differentiation of fundamental psychological types. It has always been evident that both men and women have an alternative basic approach to the world, according to whether they put their own impression on it from within or accept the impression of it which they receive from without. These two types have been fully examined and defined for the first time by Jung, who gives them the names of INTROVERT and EXTRAVERT. This distinction is not so simple as might be imagined from the common allusion to moody, thoughtful people as introverts and the hearty carefree as extraverts.

But although Jung introduces complicated subdivisions, the main distinction between introvert and extravert can be found in all activities of human life as well as in individual personalities. In religion, politics and all aspects of society the introverted and extraverted attitudes are plainly discernible, and particularly in the realm of art and literature. It is surprising that no attempt seems to have been made to consider the characters of Shakespeare in relation to their psychological type.

Goethe says that men show their character in nothing more clearly than by what they think laughable, and perhaps the somewhat technical description of the subjective and objective attitudes of introversion and extraversion can be most easily understood by a consideration of examples from humour.

The humour of the Marx Brothers is absolutely introverted. It arises, not out of their reaction to external circumstances, but from the reaction of external circumstances to them. They are too big for the situation in which they find themselves, and adapt the situation to their own purposes. The humour of the "little man", from Charlie Chaplin onwards, is just the reverse. It is dependent on his reaction to a situation which is too much for him; his actions are dictated by the situation and the humour is extraverted.

In general, introverts are capable of appreciating extraverted humour, but the opposite does not obtain. Strongly extraverted personalities do not find the Marx Brothers funny, but consider them cruel or vaguely disturbing. In modern comedy there is more often a balance between the two attitudes. Hancock is a plainly recognizable introvert, balanced by the strongly extraverted James. Hancock imagines that life is what he thinks it ought to be: James knows that it is what it always has been.

Jung carries the idea of basic introversion and extraversion a stage further, by introducing subdivisions according to the predominance of the functions of THINKING, FEELING, SENSATION and INTUITION. He regards feeling as the opposite of thinking and intuition as the opposite of sensation. Thinking and feeling are largely self-explanatory, but the other pair require further definition. In the English language the use of the word "sensation" is ambiguous, but I have been unable to find any effective substitute. I avoid the even more misleading adjective "sensitive", although I have seen it used in this connotation. It must be emphasized that Jung is referring to the unemotional use of the physical senses and the impressions received therefrom.

If thinking is the predominant function, sensation and intuition will be available as secondary functions, but feeling will be repressed in the unconscious; if feeling is predominant, thinking will similarly be repressed and the remaining functions secondary. The same position will be adopted with sensation and intuition: if either of these is predominant, the other will be repressed and the remaining functions secondary. In general, the feeling and intuitive characters are commoner amongst women and the thinking and sensation among men.

It would be attractive to equate these four principal functions with the four basic humours of the Elizabethans, but I am afraid that no such correspondence can be found. The sanguine type is recognizable as the extraverted sensation, and the melancholy as the introverted thinking, but the choleric and phlegmatic are more difficult. The choleric is extraverted and perhaps intuitive—the phlegmatic introverted but otherwise indefinable. The only clue which I can find to the missing type is Jung's description of the introverted feeling woman as one in whom "still waters run deep". The fondness of the phlegmatic for waters and fishing is the closest analogy which I can introduce.

It will be noted that there are eight possible basic personalities, all described in some detail by Jung, albeit with some obscurity partly dependent on the translation of German thoughts into English. I shall consider these basic types in their application to the characters from Shakespeare which I have selected.

# 3

# ANTONIO—THE ENDOGENOUS DEPRESSIVE

IN *The Merchant of Venice* Shakespeare sweeps straight into his subject like Brahms in his Third Symphony. As Arthur Sewell says, in the first lines both of Antonio and Orsino the character is "posed, and thus revealed". The exposition is masterly:

> In sooth I know not why I am so sad.
> It wearies me; you say it wearies you.
> But how I found it, caught it, or came by it,
> What stuff 'tis made of, whereof it is born,
> I am to learn;
> And such a want-wit sadness makes of me,
> That I have much ado to know myself.

Here is the quintessence of endogenous depression; no medical textbook has attained such brief, impressive clarity. Antonio is depressed; he is vexed with himself for feeling so apathetic; he knows he is boring his friends. But his search for a rational aetiology is fruitless. Is it some infection? Is it organic? Is it environmental? He cannot work it out. But he knows that his concentration is affected, and that his personality has in some way changed. How clumsy is a paraphrase compared with Shakespeare's poetic sketch—but he has told us all this, and more.

What of Antonio's friends—these unsubstantial figures, Salerio, Solanio and Salarino? Then there is Bassanio. Shakespeare is not prodigal of his "S" sounds except for a particular purpose. Is it sensuality which is being suggested? One is reminded of Hamlet's alliterative:

> O most wicked speed, to post
> With such dexterity to incestuous sheets.

Perhaps there is nothing in this: Shakespeare's Sebastians are not particularly sensual types.

Whenever the present equivalent of Shakespeare's merchant, the business man, falls into a state of depression, his relatives and friends unite to blame his business worries, and so with Solanio:

> Believe me, sir, had I such venture forth,
> The better part of my affections would
> Be with my hopes abroad . . .
> And every object, that might make me fear
> Misfortune to my ventures, out of doubt
> Would make me sad.

Salerio goes further—he will accept no denial:

> But tell not me: I know, Antonio
> Is sad to think upon his merchandise.

There is, of course, some dramatic irony in this, because it is these same ventures that later nearly bring Antonio to disaster.

Solanio's next gambit is obvious:

> Why, then you are in love.

Antonio's indignant denial may be important. Perhaps Solanio has unwittingly said something sensible: but, in truth, the conversation of this pair is tediously juvenile, and one marvels that a man of Antonio's natural dignity should be found in such incongruous company.

Gratiano confirms that he finds Antonio "marvellously changed", but Antonio has now thought of an answer:

> I hold the world but as the world, Gratiano;
> A stage, where every man must play a part,
> And mine a sad one.

Does this mean that Antonio's sadness is a pose, aping the scholarly melancholy fashionable at the time? Gratiano accepts this instantly, but it is clear that he is not one of Antonio's special intimates, and Antonio does not open his heart to him; he fobs him off with the answer which will be most readily acceptable.

Antonio is now left alone with Bassanio. He reminds him of his promise to relate his latest love affair. Who is the lady? But Bassanio cannot wait to answer this question. He hurries on to the business of borrowing money, supremely confident that he has only to ask for his request to be granted. And so it proves; anything which Antonio has is his:

> I pray you, good Bassanio, let me know it;
> And if it stand, as you yourself still do,
> Within the eye of honour, be assured,
> My purse, my person, my extremest means
> Lie all unlocked to your occasions.

It is true that his means are at present straitened, but Bassanio may pledge his credit to the limit.

We next meet Antonio negotiating with Shylock. He has promised to do everything in his power to help Bassanio, but this does not include curbing his tongue for the sake of diplomacy. It appears to be not so much Shylock himself who arouses his scorn and disgust as the principle of usury. There are obsessive repetitions:

> Shylock, albeit I neither lend nor borrow
> By taking nor by giving of excess,——
>           I do never use it.——
>      —And what of him—Did he take interest?——
> —Was this inserted to make interest good?——
>           —For when did friendship take
> A breed for barren metal of his friend?

One is reminded of the passionate attack on "usura" by the modern poet Ezra Pound; there is something more of feeling than reason behind it.

But Shylock does not want interest; he is prepared to forgo this for the remote chance of inflicting a humiliating and more dangerous injury. The bargain struck is too much for Bassanio, who does at least set a limit to the demands which he will make upon his friend. He has an intuitive mistrust which is not shared by Antonio, whose delight in the preservation of his principles by avoiding the payment of interest blinds him to the risk inherent in gambling with the ocean.

From this point Shakespeare seems to have forgotten the title of his play. Engrossed with his sub-plots of the caskets and Jessica's elopement, he allows Antonio to fade from the picture. Apart from a brief and rather petulant appearance at the night revels we hear of him only by report and letter during most of the second and third Acts.

Rumour of disaster to Antonio's ships gives an opportunity to assess something of his character as it appears to his friends. Solanio is concerned about the effect of the bad news:

> You were best to tell Antonio what you hear;
> Yet do not suddenly, for it may grieve him.

A kinder gentleman treads not the earth,

replies Salerio. It is evident that Bassanio's mercenary attitude is not shared by Antonio's other friends, who esteem him for his personal qualities. Salerio goes on to describe the parting of Antonio and Bassanio:

> Bassanio told him he would make some speed
> Of his return. He answered, 'Do not so;
> Slubber not business for my sake, Bassanio. . . .
> And for the Jew's bond which he hath of me,
> Let it not enter in your mind of love. . . .'
> And even there, his eye being big with tears,
> Turning his face, he put his hand behind him,
> And with affection wondrous sensible
> He wrung Bassanio's hand: and so they parted.

Solanio takes him up:

> I think he only loves the world for him.

Why this somewhat melodramatic leave-taking? Bassanio is only departing on a short voyage for his courtship, and there is no dramatic irony in the presage of disaster on the journey. Surely what lies behind this display of emotion is Antonio's intuitive knowledge that he is giving up his friend to Portia—that relations between them can never hereafter be the same. In a later chaper I shall consider whether, in its application to the Sonnets, this emotional expression of affection between males can be construed as mere artistic hyperbole, fashionable at the time.

When we next hear of Antonio, it is by a letter which interrupts the newly betrothed felicity of Bassanio and Portia. It begins: "Sweet Bassanio," perhaps not a remarkable mode of address coming from the pen of "Sweet Mr Shakespeare". The continuance is in another mood:

> My ships have all miscarried, my creditors grow cruel, my
> estate is very low, my bond to the Jew is forfeit; and since in

paying it, it is impossible I should live, all debts are cleared
between you and I, if I might but see you at my death. Notwithstanding, use your pleasure: if your love do not persuade
you to come, let not my letter.

This grave brevity, in marked contrast to the language of the
scene which it interrupts, shows a man in deep despair. An
imaginative producer will insist on small lettering for his parch-
ment—the usual theatrical flowing script would be quite out of
character.

In the scene immediately following, Antonio himself reappears. His tone to Shylock has altered:

> Hear me yet, good Shylock. . . . I pray thee, hear me
> speak.

This is by no means a cringing appeal. Antonio cannot believe
that any man, even a Jew, would really enforce a bargain of this
nature. Later he shows his innate nobility: the law must be enforced for the sake of the international reputation of the city; it
cannot be set aside to save the life of one man. The lines that
follow show the genuineness of his distressed feeling and his
insistence that only with Bassanio there can he endure the
torment of the morrow:

> These griefs and losses have so bated me,
> That I shall hardly spare a pound of flesh
> Tomorrow to my bloody creditor.
> Well, gaoler, on. Pray God, Bassanio come
> To see me pay his debt, and then I care not!

Bradley says that Antonio's melancholy makes him, not
suicidal, but indifferent to the issue of the trial. The letter to
Bassanio and this scene with Shylock and the Gaoler do not
suggest to me indifference. It is true that depression has a
damping effect on feeling of all kinds, limiting the capacity both
for enjoyment and grieving, but the presence of a completely
indifferent Antonio at the trial would rob the scene of its
dramatic effect.

Granville Barker says of Antonio that "there is conveyed in
him a better dignity than mere words can give". In contrast to
the eloquence of the plaintiff, Shylock, the defendant is certainly allotted very little to say by Shakespeare; during most of
the long court scene the actor has the difficult task of conveying

in dumb-show his reactions to the legal conflict. I am convinced that there is no indifference at any time, and the best Antonio that I have seen, Harry Andrews, portrayed a mounting agony of apprehension, leading to virtual collapse in the reaction to the final reprieve.

At first, Antonio is quietly stoical. He says of Shylock:

> I do oppose
> My patience to his fury; and am armed
> To suffer, with a quietness of spirit,
> The very tyranny and rage of his.

This is something very different both from his first contemptuous approach and from his appeal in the preceding scene. But he cannot contain himself for long:

> You may as well do anything most hard,
> As seek to soften that—than which what's harder?—
> His Jewish heart.

He must show signs of silent distress to give Bassanio his cue for:

> Good cheer, Antonio? What, man, courage yet!

To which he replies:

> I am a tainted wether of the flock,
> Meetest for death. The weakest kind of fruit
> Drops earliest to the ground; and so let me.
> You cannot better be employed, Bassanio,
> Than to live still, and write mine epitaph.

I do not take the first three lines to indicate moral taint, for reasons which will be apparent when I consider the basic character, but, rather, a fleeting reminder of the depressed mood of the opening of the play. A hint of bitterness towards his friend is evident in the final couplet.

As the legal argument develops, Antonio's impatience mounts to the agonized interruption:

> Most heartily I do beseech the court
> To give the judgement.

This is hardly a sign of indifference to the issue.

When Portia asks if he has anything to say, he has again summoned up his dignity and calm. I select from his reply the following:

> Commend me to your honourable wife.
> Tell her the process of Antonio's end.
> Say how I loved you, speak me fair in death;
> And when the tale is told, bid her be judge
> Whether Bassanio had not once a love.

Why is Bassanio's wife "honourable"? The expression in this context does not sound sincere; it reminds one of Mark Antony's sarcastic repetitions. Antonio is showing jealousy of Portia, whose love is not to be compared to his own.

I will comment no further on the court scene, except to note the bitter scorn which prompts Antonio's apparent generosity to Shylock:

> To quit the fine for one half of his goods
> I am content; so he will let me have
> The other half in use. . . .

Shylock is to lose his beloved interest, with the further wholly untenable condition that he must become a Christian.

The last Act of the play belongs to the lovers, among whom Antonio is not included. He appears out of place in the general rejoicing. Wilson Knight says that we feel that everyone would be most uncomfortable if a wife, instead of ships, were found for him in the end. But what of his melancholy? There is no mention now of that; yet his position is now no different from that at the start of the play, except that he has come through a great ordeal, perhaps effecting some kind of spiritual catharsis.

The diagnosis of Antonio's melancholy is given, without any doubt, in the first lines of the play. He is suffering from an endogenous depression. I reject any idea that the melancholy is of the fashionable whimsical kind; an interpretation on these lines can hardly survive the first scene. I am satisfied that the depressed mood has departed by the end of the play, and that, as is surely necessary for the title-role in a comedy, Antonio is left with his mental stress relieved.

There is no mystery here for the psychiatrist. Endogenous depressions arise without ascertainable cause, and they get better without specific treatment. But I have set myself the task of a more analytical approach.

First, let us consider how much of Antonio is Shakespeare's own creation. His main source is a play called *The Jew*, referred to by Stephen Gosson in his *School of Abuse*, dated 1579. In this play, the merchant Ansaldo pledges his credit so that his godson Gianetto may woo a wealthy widow, who has a compact with her suitors that, should they fail in their amatory duties, she will retain their large pecuniary deposit. She cheats them by drugging their drinks beforehand; but at Gianetto's third venture he is warned by the widow's maid, and so succeeds in his wooing. In *The Jew*, the reason for the forfeiture of the bond is Gianetto's forgetfulness, not disaster to Ansaldo's ships, and Ansaldo finally marries the sympathetic maid.

This story is a simple farcical comedy, in which the characters have little individuality. I think that, when he considered how he should use it, Shakespeare decided that there was only one circumstance in which an older man would be prepared to sacrifice so much for an unrelated younger (the "godson" is an insufficient tie), and, whether deliberately or intuitively, amended his plot to take account of this. This explains the introduction of the fresh character, Gratiano, both as a contrast to the sober Antonio and as a more suitable match for Portia's maid.

J. I. M. Stewart says that "to enrich his picture Shakespeare will borrow from a story incidents and attitudes without their causes", which were explained in the old story; but in the case of Antonio, he provides his own explanation, in implicit rather than explicit form.

L. A. G. Strong admits the endogenous nature of the depression: "A more dangerous fantasy benumbs Antonio. His picture of himself has become independent of him and produced a state of mind which is beyond his control. It arises from his unconscious mind and he can find no rational cause for it." But he makes no attempt to analyse further this "dangerous fantasy". Bradley dismisses it as merely a "pathological condition".

Stopford Brooke considers Antonio's sadness to be that of presentiment, anticipating the ordeal to come, but surely this presentiment should have told him that all would be well in the end! With perhaps more perception he also declares that "a friendship between a grave man bordering on old age and a young, gay, affectionate, wild fellow is instinct with the spirit of romance". It is true that he specifically rejects what is sometimes called a "romantic friendship", and the signs of affection in Bassanio appear subordinate to the mercenary prior to the earnest threat of Antonio's death. But the affection of Antonio for Bassanio is to me homosexual in a very broad sense.

As there is commonly an emotional and subjective bias in the consideration of this relationship, I shall endeavour to be as objective and factual as possible. Homosexuality, dismissed by many as an essentially depraved and unnatural state of vice, embraces a number of attitudes, for the majority of which the subject cannot fairly be blamed. All men have a proportion of feminine glandular substance and feminine instincts to set against their masculinity, and virtually all have homosexual feelings of some kind at some time.

Homosexuality may be repressed and unconscious to the individual, producing symptoms the cause of which he is unaware of, and which distress him without any violation of social ethics. It may be conscious but suppressed, without any overt demonstration, again harmful to the individual rather than to society as a whole. Where homosexual practices occur, the subject may be active or passive, and the respondent an elder, coeval or younger. This affects in various ways both the prognosis and the affront to society.

It is perfectly plain that Elizabethan society, as that of today, specifically regarded overt homosexual behaviour as depraved and disgusting. This view is clearly expressed by Robert Burton, and there is no reason to doubt that it was that of Shakespeare. I hasten to add that there is no evidence in the text that Antonio is conscious of sexual inversion or that Shakespeare is deliberately presenting him in this character. But it is a main part of my thesis that Shakespeare assimilated the persons in his plays to types which he observed around him, and that, intuitively, he let them control his plots according to a complexity in their nature of which he himself was only partly aware.

The quotation from Stopford Brooke apart, it is accepted by many authors that a passionate friendship between an older and a younger man—and more particularly between an older and a younger boy—may exist on a spiritual rather than a physical plane. Robert Graves and S. P. B. Mais argued this many years ago, and more recently there has been a sensitive exposition in Henri Montlhérant's play, *La Ville dont le Prince est un Enfant*. In this play the older boy sublimates his admittedly homosexual affection in a deep care and regard for the younger, prepared even to break off all communication provided that he can feel satisfied that the master who demands this is sincere and has his friend's best interests at heart.

Wilson Knight believes that Shakespeare is capable of idealizing homosexual love; he gives as an example *The Two Gentlemen of Verona*, in which masculine friendship vies with heterosexual interests.

It is difficult to extract a cause for Antonio's melancholy from the psychology of his time. Burton might consider that it was planetary influence, possibly the moon, from his interest in the voyages of his many argosies—or a simple "head melancholy" from "unevacuated seeds sending noisome vapours to the brain", another anticipation of Freud.

Lawrence Babb notes that Shakespeare's melancholics are predominantly Italian. He describes Antonio's melancholy as a "vague depression of spirits", similar to that fashionable among Renaissance scholars. As I have said before, I cannot accept this. I have seen the part played with this kind of affected insincerity, but it has never rung true at any point in the play, collapsing completely in the trial scene.

The Freudian explanation is quite simple. Antonio has not advanced beyond the homosexual phase of development, for reasons which, in the absence of any past history, hardly admit of speculation. But because of his inherent nobility and strong respect for society he cannot acknowledge his leanings, even to himself. His feelings are accordingly repressed, and his libido is insecurely attached to the object. A weaker character might regress to narcissistic behaviour or take refuge in a neurosis; but with an otherwise well-integrated personality depression is a not unnatural sequel.

The sacrifice which Antonio is prepared to make for his friend, and the scene in which it is nearly demanded in its extreme form, comprise a heroic incident in which the repressed sexuality is sublimated and turned to something higher, releasing the bands of the depression. But the sexuality of the character is not thereby changed. As Shakespeare intuitively understood, a wife for Antonio in the last Act would solve no problem. He must find other deeds to do and other worlds to conquer if he is to escape from his own nature. Today we would recommend some form of psycho-analytic treatment, but it must be admitted that the practice of this in cases of homosexuality falls short of the promise of its theory.

According to Freud, a part of the fixed homosexual character is meanness and a miserly attitude to money. Perhaps Antonio has built up his own wealth by avarice in the past, but now, with the rejection of his sexuality, he must reject all the traits that go with it; hence his overcompensating and fanatical attack on Shylock's "usury". The Freudian view does at least attempt an explanation for all the facets of the character.

With Jung, we can go a little further, without disturbing the basis of the argument. Antonio appears to be of the introverted feeling type, which is more commonly feminine. I quote from the description in Jung's *Psychological Types*:

"They are mostly silent, inaccessible and hard to understand; not infrequently their temperament is melancholic. Their outward demeanour is harmonious and inconspicuous, they reveal a delightful repose, a sympathetic parallelism, which has no desire to affect others either to impress, influence or change them in any way." Their feelings are "intensive rather than extensive . . . an intensive sympathy, because shut off from every means of expression, gains a passionate depth that embraces the misery of the world and is simply benumbed. It may possibly make an extravagant eruption, leading to some staggering act of almost heroic character, to which, however, neither the object nor the subject can find a right relation."

Where introverted feeling is the dominant characteristic, the opposite, extraverted thinking, will be pent up in the unconscious, but liable to overflow into consciousness at times. In Antonio's rejection of his own nature, with repression of feeling, this extraverted thinking becomes significant in accounting for his attitude to Shylock. Again I quote from Jung:

"This type of man (the thinking extravert) gives the deciding voice—either to the actual objective reality or to its objectively orientated, intellectual formula. By this formula are good and evil measured. . . . Just as the extraverted thinking type subordinates himself to his formula, so, for its own good, must his entourage also obey it, since the man who refuses to obey is wrong—he is resisting the World Law, and is, therefore, unreasonable, immoral, and without a conscience. His moral code forbids him to tolerate exceptions."

The final riddle of *The Merchant of Venice* is the subordinate role allotted to the title character, the only instance of this in Shakespeare's plays, apart from those in which the historical context determines the title. The common view is that Shakespeare allowed himself to be carried away by the development of character in Portia and Shylock as he swept along, relegating the "Merchant" to the background. The play is usually dated around 1596, "before the tragedy of life had laid its hand on Shakespeare" (Stopford Brooke). But this is also the generally accepted period for the early sonnets. It may be that Antonio's problem came too near to Shakespeare's own, and that, having created the character according to an intuitive perception, he became, either consciously or unconsciously, afraid to follow it in fuller detail. His artistic integrity forbade him to change it in any way, and he escaped from his dilemma by the promotion of Portia and Shylock.

# 4

## DON JOHN—THE PSYCHOPATH

ALTHOUGH, from the paucity of his lines, a minor character, Don John is the mainspring in the primary plot of *Much Ado about Nothing*. I include him in my series, partly because he represents a type as familiar today as in Shakespeare's time, and partly to demonstrate further Shakespeare's unwavering adherence to character in shaping the details of his plots.

Of Don John we do have the skeleton of a family and personal history: we know that he is a bastard, and has been newly reconciled to his half-brother, Don Pedro, presumably after some earlier peccadillo.

Warmly welcomed by Leonato, Don John's response is tepid:

> I thank you. I am not of many words, but I thank you.

We must wait until we see him with his cronies, Borachio and Conrade, before we find out what he really thinks. Conrade asks him why he is "thus out of measure sad", to which his enigmatic reply is that "there is no measure in the occasion that breeds; therefore the sadness is without limit". No more than Antonio does he understand the motives for his own behaviour:

> I cannot hide what I am. I must be sad when I have cause, and smile at no man's jests; eat when I have stomach, and wait for no man's leisure; sleep when I am drowsy, and tend to no man's business; laugh when I am merry, and claw no man in his humour.

Later it becomes apparent that he is jealous of Claudio's place in the favours of his half-brother:

> That young start-up hath all the glory of my overthrow. If I can cross him any way, I bless myself every way.

The plot that follows, to vitiate Claudio's marriage by

47

showing Hero to be promiscuous, is instigated primarily by Borachio; but he does this to assuage the jealous passion of Don
John, and his own motive is frankly mercenary—he is to receive
a fee of one thousand ducats for arranging the impersonation of
Hero by Margaret. It is apparent throughout that Borachio and
Conrade are adherents to Don John, not out of affection, but
from the hope of material advantage.

In the wedding scene Don John is his laconic self. He watches
sardonically while Claudio repulses his bride  and has a particularly brutal exit line in feigned revulsion at Hero's stricken
collapse:

> Come, let us go. These things, come thus to light,
> Smother her spirits up.

And this is the last we hear from him. Deserting his henchmen
when he finds the game is up, he takes to flight, and his capture is
announced in the concluding lines of the play. It is left to Benedick to devise "brave punishments" for him. This suggests that,
amid the general rejoicing, something humiliating rather than
with "boiling oil" in it is to be considered appropriate.

Kenneth Muir points out that in all other versions of the tale
but Shakespeare's the villain is a friend and jealous rival of the
hero. Further, in Whetstone's version—*The Rocke of Regarde*,
dated 1576—the villain, Frizaldo, marries the maid, Giletta, in
recompense for her part in abetting his deception. Why did not
Shakespeare make use of this device? He employed it later—in
the match of Sir Toby with Maria. I am sure that he presented
Don John's motive as simple malice, and refrained from including him in the happy ending, in faithfulness to a certain type of
character which he had in mind and wished to portray.

Lawrence Babb couples Don John with Aaron, of *Titus
Andronicus*, as examples of the melancholic villain in Elizabethan psychology. But the type has always existed, and is certainly common today. We used to call these men "moral de-
fectives", and now apply the more euphemistic designation—
"psychopathic personality".

Such men are incapable of affection and have no moral basis
for their behaviour. From their earliest years they have decided
that their job is to look after "number one". Characteristically
they come from broken homes, lacking both the father's example in forming right moral judgements and the mother's love

to project on to the outer world. This character is not necessarily associated with bastardy, but we can infer that Don John was brought up in the shadow of Don Pedro's condescending glory. For the want of an actual father, his elder brother has become a father-substitute, and his own position has been usurped by the supplanting Claudio.

Don John is commonly played as a man of middle age, even older than Don Pedro, which there is nothing in the text to contradict, but which seems psychologically wrong. He is surely the counterpart of the modern "Teddy-boy", insecure of his status in the world, and, though melancholy in mood, not a grave, embittered courtier.

According to the psychology of Alfred Adler, Don John feels inferior because of the circumstances of his birth, and as he has no personal qualities with which he can outvie the exuberant Don Pedro, he over-compensates by a peevish form of villainy, in which he is pathetically unsuccessful. To make a martyr of him by condign punishment would allow him to achieve his purpose of self-advertisement; therefore Benedick shows himself a good psychologist in appreciating that something humiliating will have a keener effect. The hopes of reformation in such a character are slender, and we should be left even more uncomfortable at the idea of his marriage to the unfortunate Margaret than of the grave Antonio's to the gay Nerissa.

A similar over-compensation is made by the more competent villain, Edmund, in *King Lear*, who yet shows himself capable of some spark of genuine feeling in his reaction to the deaths of Goneril and Regan. His "Yet Edmund was beloved" has some equation with Sir Andrew Aguecheek's pathetic "I was adored once."

The bastard, Philip, in *King John*, has no need to over-compensate, as his paternity, from Richard-Cœur-de-Lion, is better derived than that of his feeble brother, and he inherits from his father a true nobility of purpose.

In Jungian terms, I am sure that Don John is fundamentally an extraverted type. Feeling is strongly repressed, and thinking is the primary function. This makes him fanatical in evil doing —"religious in it", as Fabian would say.

Shakespeare's Don John may have no redeeming virtue, but he surpasses in character the merely jealous suitor of earlier versions.

4

# 5

# ORSINO—THE IMMATURE

LIKE Antonio, Orsino speaks the opening lines of the play, and seems at the beginning to be the principal male character:

> If music be the food of love, play on;
> Give me excess of it, that, surfeiting,
> The appetite may sicken, and so die.
> That strain again! It had a dying fall:
> O, it came o'er my ear like the sweet sound
> That breathes upon a bank of violets,
> Stealing and giving odour!

As Sir Andrew later says of Viola—"That youth's a rare courtier: 'rain odours', well!" But worse is to follow:

> Away before me to sweet beds of flowers!
> Love thoughts lie rich when canopied with bowers.

Flowers and odours are recurrent strains in *Twelfth Night*; the name "Viola" is redolent of Orsino's "violets", and Viola herself approaches Olivia with the "olive" in her hand.

The first impression we have of Orsino is that of a former-day Bunthorne, an affected aesthete; but this is what melancholy has brought him to, a love melancholy which is not his true character. How useful and interesting would be a past and family history of this emotionally retarded man. Although his amorous display is callow, other evidence suggests that he is about thirty. His succession to the dukedom is not recent, and it is some years since he was embroiled with Antonio in a sea-fight. The comparative ages of Orsino and Olivia seem to me of some importance, and they will be referred to again.

In the second scene of the play the Sea-Captain describes Olivia as:

> A virtuous maid, the daughter of a count
> That died some twelvemonth since; then leaving her
> In the protection of his son, her brother,
> Who shortly also died: for whose dear love,
> They say, she hath abjured the sight
> And company of men.

There is also evidence from the Captain that Orsino is:

> A noble duke, in nature as in name.

Viola resolves to serve this duke in the guise of a eunuch, although, as Coleridge points out, when she arrives at his court it is as an ordinary page-in-attendance. The progress she makes with Orsino in the short space of three days arouses the jealousy of Valentine:

> If the Duke continue his favours towards you, Cesario, you are like to be much advanced: he hath known you but three days, and already you are no stranger.

It is clear that the Duke enjoys the company of his young attendant. He has already taken Viola deeply into his confidence:

> Thou know'st no less than all. I have unclasped
> To thee the book even of my secret soul.

In a passage of dramatic irony he shows himself unconsciously aware of Viola's femininity:

> For they shall yet belie thy happy years
> That say thou art a man. Diana's lip
> Is not more smooth and rubious; thy small pipe
> Is as the maiden's organ, shrill and sound,
> And all is semblative a woman's part.

In sending Viola as his ambassador of love Orsino is following a practice common among the nobility of his time; but it does seem curious that this love-sick lord should make no active attempt to bring his loved one within his sight until the final scene of the play.

In the course of Viola's first embassage we learn something about Orsino from another point of view—that of Olivia:

> Your lord does know my mind: I cannot love him.
> Yet I suppose him virtuous, know him noble,
> Of great estate, of fresh and stainless youth;
> In voices well divulged, free, learned and valiant;
> And in dimension and the shape of nature

> A gracious person: but yet I cannot love him.
> He might have took his answer long ago.

Wilson Knight sees Orsino as a barbaric figure, bear-like from the derivation of his name, and definitely not a juvenile lead. A man of thirty might be still "of fresh and stainless youth", but the rest of Olivia's description is hardly barbaric.

In Act II, after the nocturnal caterwauling of the comedians, Shakespeare returns to his main plot in one of the most poignant scenes in any of his plays. The atmosphere is vibrant with the sweet sadness of music, so apt, in Burton's view, for the relief of love melancholy, and amid which the superficial affectation of the old love is conquered by the quiet, deep sincerity of the new.

The Duke calls for music. As the first notes sound he detaches Viola from the assembled court:

> Come hither, boy. If ever thou shalt love,
> In the sweet pangs of it remember me;
> For such as I am all true lovers are,
> Unstaid and skittish in all motions else,
> Save in the constant image of the creature
> That is beloved.

I think the audience will infer the exact opposite. Except when thinking of Olivia, Orsino shows himself as a well integrated and reasonable person: It is only in his love that he is "unstaid and skittish".

Viola is affected by the music:

> It gives a very echo to the seat
> Where love is throned.

With a flash of intuition Orsino becomes aware of something deeper:

>                   Thou dost speak masterly.
> My life upon't, young though thou art, thine eye
> Hath stayed upon some favour that it loves.
> Hath it not, boy?

VIOLA:                   A little, by your favour.

DUKE: What kind of woman is't?

VIOLA:                   Of your complexion.

DUKE: She is not worth thee then. What years, i'faith?

VIOLA: About your years, my lord.

DUKE: Too old, by heaven. Let still the woman take
> An elder than herself: so wears she to him,
> So sways she level in her husband's heart.

> For, boy, however we do praise ourselves,
> Our fancies are more giddy and unfirm,
> More longing, wavering, sooner lost and won
> Than women's are.

This is surely Shakespeare's own philosophy, given an ironic touch by the circumstance of his own marriage with an older woman. Dramatic irony is added to this if Olivia should be older than Orsino, which I am convinced is Shakespeare's intention.

The Duke's next quatrain holds an interest beyond its poetic value:

> Then let thy love be younger than thyself,
> Or thy affection cannot hold the bent.
> For women are as roses, whose fair flower
> Being once displayed, doth fall that very hour.

Robert Burton makes precisely the same observation in his chapter on love melancholy. Remarking that an old man may marry a young maid, but not vice versa, he proceeds: "A virgin, as the Poet holds, a desirous and sportive girl, is like a flower, a Rose withered on a sudden." If the *Anatomy of Melancholy* had not been published after Shakespeare's death, critics would be assuring us that Shakespeare had studied Robert Burton. The evidence is at least as strong as that provided by Kenneth Muir and Dover Wilson to show that he had read Timothy Bright before writing *Hamlet*. It is possible that Burton had attended a performance of *Twelfth Night*, but more likely that both writers drew their inspiration direct from the Roman poet, Ausonius.

The exquisite melancholy of the song that follows is enhanced by the indifference of the normally mercenary Feste to his fee for singing it:

> DUKE: There's for thy pains.
> FESTE: No pains, sir. I take pleasure in singing, sir.

The magic is swiftly dispelled when Orsino returns to his obsession:

> Once more, Cesario,
> Get thee to yond same sovereign cruelty;
> Tell her my love, more noble than the world,
> Prizes not quantity of dirty lands.
>
> . . . . . . . . . . . . . . . . . . . . . .
> But 'tis that miracle and queen of gems
> That nature pranks her in attracts my soul.

Not only does the bombastic hyperbole return, but Orsino completely contradicts what he has just been telling Viola of the instability of men in love, compared with women:

> There is no woman's sides
> Can bide the beating of so strong a passion
> As love doth give my heart; no woman's heart
> So big, to hold so much: they lack retention.
> Alas, their love may be called appetite—
> . . . . . . . . . . . . . . Make no compare
> Between that love a woman can bear me
> And that I owe Olivia.

A little later we have again the contrast of Viola's simple sincerity:

> We men may say more, swear more: but indeed
> Our shows are more than will; for still we prove
> Much in our vows, but little in our love.

After this scene the main plot is allowed to rest until the last Act. Meanwhile we see no more of Orsino, but the plots are connected by the tenuous device of involving Viola in the mock duel with Sir Andrew. This scene effects in me almost as much embarrassment as the baiting of the "lunatic", Malvolio. Either Viola must step out of character or we must witness a scene played in two separate styles. I shall not readily forget the agonized terror projected by Peggy Ashcroft at this point. This did not fit the mood of the scene, but seems to me necessary for sustaining the character, unless it can be shown that Viola, with her alert intelligence, is not persuaded of the serious nature of the duel.

When Orsino reappears, in the last Act, his cheerful exchange of badinage with Feste suggests that his melancholy has been dispelled. Perhaps this is because he has at last plucked up the courage to tackle Olivia for himself. But before she arrives some further light is shed upon his essential nature by his confrontation of Antonio:

> That face of his I do remember well.
> . . . . . . . . . . . . . . . . . . . .
> A baubling vessel was he captain of,
> . . . . . . . . . . . . . . . . . . . .
> With which such scathful grapple did he make
> With the most noble bottom of our fleet
> That very envy and the tongue of loss
> Cried fame and honour on him.

Here is an opponent generous in defeat. We also learn that a nephew of his lost a leg in the same battle, confirming that Orsino cannot be a very young man unless he had a brother or sister much older than himself.

The entrance of Olivia instantly resurrects Orsino's hyperbolic language:

> Here comes the Countess: now heaven walks on earth.

Her curt rejection spurs him to the following rodomontade:

> Why should I not, had I the heart to do it,
> Like to the Egyptian thief at point of death,
> Kill what I love?—a savage jealousy
> That sometime savours nobly. But hear me this:
> Since you to non-regardance cast my faith,
> And that I partly know the instrument
> That screws me from my true place in your favour,
> Live you the marble-breasted tyrant still;
> But this your minion, whom I know you love,
> And whom, by heaven I swear, I tender dearly,
> Him will I tear out of that cruel eye
> Where he sits crowned in his master's spite.
> Come, boy, with me; my thoughts are ripe in mischief:
> I'll sacrifice the lamb that I do love,
> To spite a raven's heart within a dove.

Wilson Knight sees Orsino as ruthless in his passion, prepared to kill Viola when he finds that she has betrayed him. I have quoted the passage in full to show the patent insincerity of the language. Orsino has no more intention of going beyond ranting words than he has a true belief in a love "as hungry as the sea". Unconsciously, of course, his anger is inspired by the threatened loss, not of Olivia, which has always been inevitable, but of Viola herself. When he appreciates that this loss too is apparently irrevocable, he shows that, in his true love, he can match Viola's simple dignity of speech:

> O thou dissembling cub! what wilt thou be
> When time hath sown a grizzle on thy case?
> Or will not else thy craft so quickly grow
> That thine own trip shall be thine overthrow?
> Farewell, and take her; but direct thy feet
> Where thou and I henceforth may never meet.

It is true that at the final "discovery" Viola catches something of Orsino's lost hyperbole:

DUKE:  Boy, thou hast said to me a thousand times
Thou never shouldst love woman like to me.
VIOLA:  And all those sayings will I over-swear;
And all those swearings keep as true in soul
As doth that orbed continent the fire
That severs day from night.

But this springs from a natural surfeit of sudden bliss, becoming in the newly-revealed woman. As L. A. G. Strong suggests, Viola will make a man of Orsino yet.

According to Leslie Hotson, the name Orsino was chosen by Shakespeare in honour of Virginio Orsino, Duke of Bracciano, "the most brilliant nobleman of his day, who was Ambassador from the Vatican to the Spanish court and was entertained by Queen Elizabeth at the time *Twelfth Night* may well have been performed for the first time, in 1601." Virginio Orsino was twenty-eight at the time; he had married Flavia, grand-niece of Pope Sixtus V, at the age of sixteen, and had six children by 1601, including twins, a boy and a girl. His character is described by Cardinal d'Osset as "of very great worth and valour, but a gentle soul". His family history is interesting. According to Webster's *The White Devil* his father strangled his mother out of jealousy and later arranged the murder of Vittoria Accorambona's husband so that he could make her his second wife. Soon after this his father died, and his stepmother was murdered by a cousin to ensure the descent of the Orsino fortune to Virginio. After the death of his father, Virginio was brought up by an uncle to whom he was much attached. He would have liked to marry his cousin, a year younger than himself, but was obliged to turn to Flavia because of the need for a political alliance. In spite of this there is no suggestion that the marriage was not happy.

If Shakespeare really had in mind the Duke Virginio Orsino for his prototype there is ample material in the past history for the development of a neurosis; but, even if it is correct that he used the name in honour of Elizabeth's distinguished visitor, I am sure that the character is of his own invention. The essential nobility behind the mask of the love melancholy enhances at least the plausibility of Professor Hotson's thesis, but does not help us in the elucidation of Orsino's emotional state.

In the various versions of the main plot of *Twelfth Night* available to Shakespeare, of which the Italian *Gl'Inganni* is the nearest, the character corresponding to Viola is already in love with the Duke at the start of the play, and deliberately disguises herself to serve him. The love-sickness of Orsino is of Shakespeare's own contrivance.

In Elizabethan terms, the psychology of Orsino is well understood, following closely the description of love melancholy given by Robert Burton—"which enervates the bravest soldiers and most generous spirits". Orsino's love for Olivia is certainly immoderate in its expression; perhaps Burton would say that he was born under the influence of Venus. He analyses the steps of unruly love as they proceed from sight, speech and company to kissing and handling. In the case of Orsino, his love for Olivia hardly progresses to speech, whereas the company of Viola breeds the exquisite melancholy of Act II, Scene 4.

Burton advises the introduction of a more suitable love object, and considers marriage the best cure for unruly love. Lawrence Babb also mentions blood-letting, exercise, study and diet as remedies in Elizabethan literature. Sleep, gaiety, music and travel may also in various cases be recommended. Most of these cures are inspired by Ovid's *De Remedio Amoris*.

Babb says that Orsino does not seem to suffer greatly from his love melancholy, and finds Shakespeare sceptical about the whole idea.

The self-imposed seven years' mourning of Olivia is in itself an interesting study. Most of the critics agree that this is a transparent excuse for rejecting an unwelcome suit; I think there is some evidence that the disturbance goes much deeper. Olivia does not rebuff Orsino because he is personally unacceptable; she is frigid and would have behaved in the same way with another suitor. Freud says that women frequently have an unconscious aversion from sexual interests—as something forbidden. I picture Olivia's brother as a much older, dominating man, to whom she has formed an attachment so deep that her libido is fixed. To her a mature man is a brother-substitute and therefore not acceptable as a sexual partner; her desire can only be awakened by a very young man, to whom no taboo will be attached.

This leads to the vexed question of Olivia's age. Shakespeare's contemporary, John Manningham, refers in his diary to a play performed at the Middle Temple "like *Gl'Inganni*" from which he received the impression that Olivia was a widow. Productions

today usually present Olivia as a young girl, possibly with the
idea of making her marriage to Sebastian more plausible. Margaret Webster, one of the few critics from the theatrical world,
is emphatic on this point, but I cannot agree with it.

I do not adopt the common argument that Olivia is clearly
an authoritative figure in competent control of her household; a
young girl who had early lost her mother might well have
attained this kind of competence. But for me it is essential for
the understanding both of Orsino's and her own attitude to sex
and marriage that we should regard her as a mature woman,
slightly older than Orsino himself. Even before I attempted to
analyse the reasons for this I was always conscious of something incongruous in productions presenting Olivia as a young
and sportive creature.

Orsino's counterpart is common enough today. Characteristically these men have dominating mothers. In Freudian terms,
the fixation of the libido on the mother may effect one of two
results. Either an object similar to the mother may be sought, or
the feminine character may be decisively rejected. Freud implies
that, in the second case, homosexuality results, either from a
feeling of incestuous guilt attached to a female partner or from
the delayed shift of the libido from the mother to a homosexual
object, which should have been the normal succession in
childhood.

I think that this can be presented in simpler terms. The
domination of the mother may either be accepted or rejected. If
accepted, a partner of similar dominating type, often older, is
sought; if rejected, a bisexual attitude is taken up—the man
wants a woman without her complex feminine psychology. The
nearest to this may be the adolescent boy or the very young,
inexperienced girl.

Shakespeare expresses something of this dilemma in his
twentieth Sonnet:

> A woman's face with Nature's own hand painted
> Hast thou, the master-mistress of my passion;
> A woman's gentle heart, but not acquainted
> With shifting change, as is false woman's fashion.

Tennessee Williams has explored the less attractive territories
of this particular situation in his terrifying play, *Suddenly,
Last Summer*, in which the dominating mother tolerates and

abets the abnormal sexual outlets of her son in order to preserve him unmarried for herself.

In the case of Orsino, I imagine that his mother is newly dead and that he is in process of freeing himself from her shackles. This places him in an unstable, ambivalent mood. Olivia is clearly a dominating type, as shown by her attitude to her uncle and domestic staff, and I have given reasons for assuming her to be mature. Viola, the girl-boy, exactly meets Orsino's need of a partner to rescue him from his dotage on a mother-substitute. At present his immaturity is matched by her own youthful psycho-sexual development, and as they grow older he can be assured that she will "wear to him" and so "sway level in her husband's heart".

Orsino's psychological type is difficult to define. He is clearly introverted, and his primary function seems to be something between thinking and intuition. The repressed functions of feeling and sensation, being extraverted, are responsible for the abrupt change of language and behaviour when his attention is focused on Olivia.

Jung describes the introverted thinking type as: "generally stubborn, headstrong and unamenable to influence in the pursuit of his ideas. . . . His suggestibility to personal influences is in strong contrast to this. . . . By his wider circle he is accounted inconsiderate and domineering. But the better one knows him, the more favourable one's judgment becomes, and his nearest friends are well aware how to value his intimacy. . . . The various measures of self-defence, the curious protective obstacles with which such people are wont to surround themselves, are sufficiently familiar. . . . A vague dread of the other sex belongs to this category."

The purely introverted intuitive type tends to produce mystical dreamers and artistic cranks, but it is with the unconscious attributes of this type that Orsino has some affinity. Jung says that: "the unconscious personality may best be described as an extraverted sensation type of a rather low and primitive order. Impulsiveness and unrestraint are the characters of this sensation, combined with an extraordinary dependence on the sense impression. . . . But if, through a forced exaggeration of the conscious attitude, a complete subordination to the inner perception should develop, the unconscious becomes in opposition, giving rise to compulsive sensations

whose excessive dependence on the object is in frank conflict
with the conscious attitude. The form of neurosis is a compulsion neurosis exhibiting . . . partly compulsive ties to definite
persons or other objects."

Jung's psychological theory is admittedly complex, but I
think that Orsino's compulsive fixation on Olivia is derived
from an unconscious personality of the type described above.

The importance of Orsino's character to the plot and structure
of the play rests in his early disappearance from it. As with
Antonio in *The Merchant of Venice*, Shakespeare first presents
him as the most important figure—only to drop him abruptly
after the second Act. It has been suggested that he became
engrossed in the character of Malvolio, as in that of Shylock,
and found that he could not fit Orsino into the extended development of the secondary plot. But there may be more to it
than that. Both Shylock and Malvolio are characters observed
and reported on from without. I am sure that there is a good
deal of Shakespeare himself in Orsino: his observations on
marriage partnership seem to come from the heart, and can
hardly be dissociated from his own union with a woman six
years older than himself.

My view is that, as with Antonio. Shakespeare unconsciously
found it painful to probe deeper into Orsino's true personality.
It is surely significant that the character is dropped after the
most moving and intimate scene. Not until he had refreshed
himself with gusts of pure light-hearted farce from Sir Toby and
his companions could Shakespeare face the task of concluding
his primary plot by the abrupt revelation to Orsino of Viola's
true sex. There is even then no return to the intimacy of the
earlier scenes, and we are denied any glimpse of Orsino alone
with his "mistress and his fancy's queen".

It is interesting to note that T. W. Baldwin, in his recon-
struction of the cast-list of the plays, allots the part of Orsino to
Burbadge, established by then as the leading actor in succession
to Augustine Phillips, who presumably played Malvolio. If this
is correct, Orsino was accepted by Shakespeare's company as
the leading part. By contrast, Baldwin does not dispute that
Burbadge played Shylock in *The Merchant of Venice*, and allots
Antonio to Cundall.

# 6

## JAQUES—THE INVOLUTIONAL

THE character of Jaques in *As You Like It* is Shakespeare's own conception of the melancholy philosopher, owing nothing to the sources from which he derives his play.

Jaques is introduced at second hand, at the beginning of Act II, by an account of his behaviour given to the exiled Duke by one of his attendant lords. The Duke regrets the necessity to kill the native deer for food, receiving the answer:

> Indeed, my lord,
> The melancholy Jaques grieves at that,
> And, in that kind, swears you do more usurp
> Than doth your brother that hath banished you.

The lord gives a touching description of the flight of a wounded stag, which:

> Much marked of the melancholy Jaques,
> Stood on th'extremest verge of the swift brook,
> Augmenting it with tears.
>
> DUKE:                            But what said Jaques?
> Did he not moralize this spectacle?
> LORD: O, yes, into a thousand similes.
> First, for his weeping into the needless stream:
> "Poor deer," quoth he, "thou mak'st a testament
> As worldlings do, giving thy sum of more
> To that which had too much." Then, being there alone,
> Left and abandoned of his velvet friends:
> " 'Tis right," quoth he, "thus misery doth part
> The flank of company." Anon a careless herd,
> Full of the pasture, jumps along by him
> And never stays to greet him: "Ay," quoth Jaques,
> "Sweep on, you fat and greasy citizens;
> 'Tis just the fashion. Wherefore do you look
> Upon that poor and broken bankrupt there?"

> Thus most invectively he pierceth through
> The body of the country, city, court,
> Yea, and of this our life, swearing that we
> Are mere usurpers, tyrants and what's worse,
> To fright the animals and to kill them up
> In their assigned and native dwelling-place.

Thus his companions leave the melancholy Jaques—"weeping and commenting upon the sobbing deer".

Again I quote at length, because of Shakespeare's habit of setting a character with his first speech, in this case with the minor variation of putting the words into the mouth of an observer. From this we learn that Jaques is a critical student of human nature, decrying the pattern of organized society, but not without feelings capable of being moved by the plight of a wounded animal.

When first seen in person, Jaques is demanding an encore to a song from Amiens. Amiens objects that this will make him more melancholy—to which he replies:

> I thank it. More, I prithee, more. I can suck melancholy out
> of a song, as a weasel sucks eggs.

His melancholy is plainly self-induced.

Jaques adds to the song a verse of his own composition:

> If it do come to pass
> That any man turn ass,
> Leaving his wealth and ease
> A stubborn will to please,
> Ducdame, ducdame, ducdame,
> Here shall he see
> Gross fools as he,
> And if he will come to me.

This verse establishes that his exile is voluntary—now causing humorous and not very sincere regret.

It is not long before Jaques reappears in a state of most unmelancholy excitement engendered by his first meeting with Touchstone. He is struck with the idea that he has missed his vocation, avid to desert his amateur railing for the more polished folly of the professional:

> Invest me in my motley: give me leave
> To speak my mind, and I will through and through
> Cleanse the foul body of th' infected world
> If they will patiently receive my medicine.

The Duke immediately snubs him:

> Most mischievous foul sin, in chiding sin,
> For thou thyself hast been a libertine,
> As sensual as the brutish sting itself;
> And all th' embossed sores and headed evils,
> That thou with license of free foot hast caught,
> Wouldst thou disgorge into the general world.

This passage appears to be much relied on by the critics as the key to Jaques' past character. I quote from H. B. Charlton: "Jaques has been corrupted into superciliousness by cultivating superiority and habituating himself to contemplative mockery and polite persiflage. He patronizes humanity, but there is no love. He thinks he knows himself and the world; but, perhaps because he fled from both to purge himself of his earlier sensuality and his libertinage, his knowledge is superficial, impressive no doubt to the hearer by its philosophic seeming, but inadequate in its findings and distorted in its values."

I think too much can be read into the Duke's remarks. He is on jocular terms with Jaques and may be only repeating some earlier humorous self-appraisal by the latter. I prefer Helen Gardner's view of Jaques as the "quintessential only child"—a lonely introverted character difficult to envisage on a gay debauch.

The dissertation on The Seven Ages of Man is surely an example of Shakespeare's precise observation put into the mouth of a character apt to express it. The satirical content is not unkindly, and I do not see in the subsequent entrance of Orlando bearing Adam on his back an immediate rebuke to the cynicism of Jaques; this is merely a telling dramatic contrast, repeated immediately by the song condemning man's ingratitude.

J. I. M. Stewart describes "All the world's a stage" as a false observation, because real life and the stage representation of it are quite different. Now I agree that if a character in real life made such an observation it would be untrue, but Jaques is himself a character in a play, and therefore his view of the world outside the play in which he appears is part of the character given to him by the author; it cannot be judged in terms of truth and falsity.

Kenneth Muir points out that this speech is a variation on the motto of the new theatre to which Shakespeare and his company had just moved. This lends support to the conception of Jaques

as a commentating mouthpiece with views on life at the pessi-
mistic extreme of Shakespeare's own, balanced by the optimism
of the other commentator, Touchstone.

Every critic has drawn attention to the balance between
Touchstone and Jaques. Miss Gardner describes Touchstone as
the parodist who must love what he parodies, and Jaques as the
cynic who cannot be converted from melancholy because he
likes himself as he is. Neither of these two helps to advance the
plot. They cannot therefore be considered solely in relation to
other characters in the play, but as the link between the poet
and the audience. All the plays have one or more of these
"chorus" figures, but it so happens that Jaques is the only one
to be considered in my series.

A feature in *As You Like It*, first noted by Ulrici, is the sym-
metrical arrangement of the characters in pairs. Apart from the
obvious conjunctions, such as that of Jaques and Touchstone,
different characters become paired in different ways. There is the
nominal pairing of the two Olivers and the two Jaques, an
accident peculiar to *As You Like It*, and there are temporary
pairings—such as the following between Jaques and Orlando:

> JAQUES: I thank you for your company; but, good faith, I
>     had as lief been myself alone.
> ORLANDO: And so had I; but yet, for fashion's sake,
>     I thank you too for your society.
> JAQUES: God buy you. Let's meet as little as we can.
> ORLANDO: I do desire we may be better strangers.
> JAQUES: I pray you, mar no more trees with writing love
>     songs in their barks.
> ORLANDO: I pray you, mar no more of my verses with
>     reading them ill-favouredly.
> JAQUES: Rosalind is your love's name?
> ORLANDO: Yes, just.
> JAQUES: I do not like her name.
> ORLANDO: There was no thought of pleasing you when she
>     was christened.
> JAQUES: What stature is she of?
> ORLANDO: Just as high as my heart.
> JAQUES: You are full of pretty answers. Have you not been
>     acquainted with goldsmiths' wives, and conned them
>     out of rings?
> ORLANDO: Not so; but I answer you right painted cloth,
>     from whence you have studied your questions.

JAQUES: You have a nimble wit: I think 'twas made of
    Atalanta's heels. Will you sit down with me? And we
    two will rail against our mistress the world, and all
    our misery.

ORLANDO: I will chide no breather in the world but myself,
    against whom I know most faults.

JAQUES: The worst fault you have is to be in love.

ORLANDO: 'Tis a fault I will not change for your best virtue.
    I am weary of you.

JAQUES: By my troth, I was seeking for a fool when I
    found you.

ORLANDO: He is drowned in the brook. Look but in, and
    you shall see him.

JAQUES: There I shall see mine own figure.

ORLANDO: Which I take to be either a fool or a cipher.

JAQUES: I'll tarry no longer with you. Farewell, good
    Signior Love.

ORLANDO: I am glad of your departure. Adieu, good
    Monsieur Melancholy.

The symbolism of the brook suggests Narcissus communing
with himself, and I find in this duologue two aspects of a single
character, the conscious and the unconscious. Jaques's conscious type is that of the thinking introvert. Again I quote from
Jung:

"His judgement appears cold, obstinate, arbitrary and inconsiderate, simply because he is related less to the object than
to the subject. One can feel nothing in it that might possibly
confer a higher value on the object; it always seems to go beyond
the object, leaving behind it a flavour of a certain subjective
superiority. Courtesy, amiability and friendliness may be
present, but often with a particular quality suggesting a certain
uneasiness, which betrays an ulterior aim, namely, the dis-
arming of an opponent, who must at all costs be pacified and
set at ease lest he prove a disturbing element. . . . Either he is
taciturn or he falls among people who cannot understand him;
whereupon he proceeds to gather further proof of the un-
fathomable stupidity of man. . . . Foreign influences are
eliminated; he becomes more unsympathetic to his peripheral
world, and therefore more dependent upon his intimates. . . .
His originally fertilizing ideas become destructive, because
poisoned by a kind of sediment of bitterness. His struggle
against the influences emanating from the unconscious increases

with his external isolation, until gradually this begins to cripple him. A still greater isolation must surely protect him from the unconscious influences, but as a rule this only takes him deeper into the conflict which is destroying him from within."

The duologue finds Jaques at war with his unconscious influences, represented by Orlando. As thinking is his primary function, so feeling of a primitive extraverted kind is repressed in his unconscious, and it is this extraverted feeling which is bubbling up in Orlando. Love, and the feeling associated with it, is the arch-enemy which Jaques must keep from his conscious mind at all costs. He makes a final appeal to Orlando to join him in railing against "our mistress the world", but Orlando is a well-integrated personality: he knows, like Cassius, that any fault in his life lies not in his stars but in himself. Jaques, incapable of self-criticism, retires defeated in argument, but victorious in the impregnability of his conscious mind to the incursion of feeling from the unconscious.

It may be objected that Orlando is the leading character in the play, to whom Jaques is in inferior relation, and that any symbolism should be analysed in its application to Orlando's psyche. This can well be done on a Freudian basis. According to this, Jaques represents Orlando's super-ego in this scene, a critical figure, part God, part father substitute, with whom Orlando in love must commune to persuade himself of the reasonable basis for his feeling. But the super-ego is soon dismissed, as must always happen. An attempt to put love on a logical basis can only be a feeble rationalization; for by its very nature love is the antithesis of reason.

The two interpretations are not contradictory, but may be considered as complementary. Shakespeare is wedded to no one psychological theory, but embodies in his works the fundamental truths which are common to all.

The relation between Jaques and Touchstone is psychologically similar. Touchstone represents the extraverted character which Jaques would like to be—not exactly complementary, because intuition is Touchstone's primary function. But if we accept the past indulgence of Jaques in promiscuous adventures abroad, the function secondary to his predominant thinking will be sensation, which postulates at least the partial repression of intuition.

At his next appearance Jaques shows himself more humane in action than in observation. Despite his cynical disparagement of love, he is shocked that the wedding of Touchstone and Audrey should be hastily contrived, through the offices of a divine of dubious reputation:

> And will you, being a man of your breeding, be married under a bush like a beggar? Get you to church, and have a good priest that can tell you what marriage is. This fellow will but join you together as they join wainscot; then one of you will prove a shrunk panel, and, like green timber, warp, warp.

Touchstone takes him up with an aside:

> I am not in the mind but I were better to be married of him than another. For he is not like to marry me well; and not being well married, it will be a good excuse for me hereafter to leave my wife.

Jaques's pessimism has been instanced in his parting allegation that Touchstone's "loving voyage is but two months victualled", for which this aside from Touchstone seems to provide ample justification.

Jaques appears anxious for the good opinion of Rosalind, and from his attempted self-appraisal during his one short duologue with her we are provided with his own view of his melancholy:

> I have neither the scholar's melancholy, which is emulation; nor the musician's, which is fantastical; nor the soldier's, which is ambitious; nor the lawyer's, which is politic; nor the lady's, which is nice; nor the lover's, which is all these: but it is a melancholy of mine own, compounded of many simples, extracted from many objects; and indeed the sundry contemplation of my travels, in which my often rumination wraps me in a most humorous sadness.

In fact, this speech tells us little about Jaques himself, but a good deal about Elizabethan psychological theory, further subdividing melancholic types to complement Burton and Bright's description of the astrological and humoral varieties.

H. B. Charlton is severely critical of Jaques at this point, saying that "his psycho-analytic formula of his own melancholy is nothing but the covering up of moral deficiency by a pseudoscientific explanation of it". Arthur Sewell, more tolerant, describes Jaques as "one of those characters for whom an audience is necessary. He has a high degree of self-awareness, giving evidence that there is something of Shakespeare in him."

I do not credit Jaques with much personal insight, but it is not his task in the play to explain himself; his imperfect account of his own melancholy does not to me argue moral deficiency. As a commentator he is the link between the author and his audience, and I agree that his views are often those of Shakespeare. If then it is true, as has been suggested by many critics, that the name "Rosalind", or "Rosaline" had a special significance for Shakespeare, surely her opinion of Jaques must be important in the assessment of his character. Here it follows:

> A traveller! By my faith you have great reason to be sad. I fear you have sold your own lands to see other men's. Then to have seen so much, and to have nothing, is to have rich eyes and poor hands.

Jaques replies, with unusual sententiousness:

> Yes, I have gained my experience.

To which Rosalind retorts:

> And your experience makes you sad. I had rather have a fool to make me merry than experience to make me sad; and to travel for it too! . . . Farewell, Monsieur Traveller. Look you lisp and wear strange suits; disable all the benefits of your own country; be out of love with your nativity and almost chide God for making you that countenance you are; or I will scarce think you have swam in a gondola.

Stopford Brooke says that Jaques is vain and hurt by Rosalind's snubbing, which Shakespeare intended should cure him of his melancholy, but, according to the stage directions, he is off-stage before she has reached the most telling part; his abrupt exit is precipitated by the appearance of Orlando, whose love-struck speech is alien music to him.

In any case, Rosalind's mockery is light-hearted and mostly directed against the foreign fashions which Jaques does not affect. She cannot believe him to have been a traveller, because he has not picked up the traveller's affectations. In truth she can pierce the mask of melancholy to expose the heart beneath.

Despite his verbal acidity Jaques is capable of true feeling and kindness. The character is posed in its first presentation: Jaques is sorry for the deer and weeps. Later, despite his inveighing against the state of love, he sees to it that Touchstone and Audrey are wed with due formality.

The merciless snubbing of Jaques might be in the character of the false dark lady of the Sonnets, but does not accord with the kindly wit of Shakespeare's Rosalind. The choice of name may be from some unconscious chord of memory, but the essential character of the dark lady is inconstancy, the reverse of what may be observed in the three gay heroines, Portia, Viola and Rosalind, instanced in Frank Harris's catalogue of Shakespeare's women.

Jaques exhibits no sign of feeling hurt or snubbed after this encounter. A brief musical interlude shows him in his normal spirits, after which he does not appear until the final scene. Here he is in excellent humour, full of admiration for the wit of Touchstone, and studying that he may emulate it.

Shakespeare is not at his best in the unravelling of the strands of his comedies at their conclusion, and there is much that appears crude and hastily contrived. In the final scene of *Cymbeline* the repetitive exclamations of the puzzled king become embarrassing as detail after detail of the plot is wound up and explicated; Bernard Shaw's claim for the superiority of his amended version is not without justification.

In *As You Like It*, the sudden repentance of the usurping Duke is hardly credible, but, as the character is imperfectly developed in the first Act, Shakespeare is not in this instance proving false to his own creation. But the shedding by Jaques of his melancholy to become a courtier in the new régime would have been a flagrant breach of characterization, of which he could not be guilty. Not so simply nor so quickly can the conflict in Jaques's psyche be resolved. Perhaps a study of Duke Frederick's problem will help to solve his own: he cannot miss this chance of interrogating a repentant sinner.

The leave-taking of Jaques is generous and dignified:

| | |
|---|---|
| (To Duke Senior) | You to your former honour I bequeath, |
| | Your patience and your virtue well deserve it; |
| (To Orlando) | You to a love that your true faith doth merit; |
| (To Oliver) | You to your land, and love, and great allies; |
| (To Silvius) | You to a long and well-deserved bed; |

(To Touchstone)    And you to wrangling, for thy loving voyage
Is but for two months victualled. So, to your
pleasures.
I am for other than for dancing measures.

I believe that this is Shakespeare himself bidding farewell to
the characters in his play, which he must now leave to trace the
path that leads through the great tragedies to the final dramas of
sin and repentance, that themselves explore the problem of
Duke Frederick and the reasons for his change of heart.

Superficially, it is easy to see in Jaques the melancholy
scholar of the Renaissance period. Lawrence Babb says that in
Elizabethan literature the melancholy man is accorded dignity
and respect; but he stigmatizes Jaques as morose, cynical and
rude, though he has to admit his humanity expressed in his
sorrow for the deer. As a traveller Jaques might well have ac-
quired the melancholic mood fashionable in Italy, but Rosalind
specifically acquits him of this affectation. Yet, the melancholy
is of his own choosing. He is in no sense a case for a psychiatrist; his symptoms neither disturb himself nor cause harm to
other people. Babb suggests that he has difficulty in sleeping,
on the slender evidence of the following:

> I'll go sleep if I can: if I cannot, I'll rail against all the first-
> born of Egypt.

But we receive the impression that he will rather enjoy being
unable to sleep, in complete contrast to the insomnia of the
pathological melancholic.

Neither is he in any way neurotic. He has rejected the outside
world, but not from a failure to adjust himself to its requirements. He is no longer interested in material affairs—his
criticism of others is abstract and general rather than concrete
and specific. He is concerned with what they think and say
rather than with what they do; in other words he is engaging
himself with the spiritual side of man's nature. He perceives
that to do this successfully requires a quality of detached and
humorous intuition which he himself does not possess, but
which is the basis of the natural genius of Touchstone.

Freud would say that Jaques has a strongly developed super-
ego, which causes him to project his own failings on to others,
and criticize in them faults of which he himself is unconsciously
guilty. But this is not the total significance of the character.

According to the theory of Jung, the melancholy of Jaques is his persona, the façade which he presents to the outer world, covering the deeper layers of the ego, both conscious and unconscious. This is a perfectly satisfactory persona, giving him a useful and honoured place with the Duke and with the company that he has chosen. The irruption of the disturbing elements from outside, in the persons of Rosalind, Celia, Orlando and Touchstone, presents new problems to the enclosed community of Arden; but they also enrich and revitalize a life that was becoming stagnant—providing Jaques with new material to aid his spiritual search, but drawing also from him his contribution to the solution of their own immediate psychological disturbances, even though this be by a critical rather than by an openly adjuvatory approach.

In *Modern Man in Search of a Soul*, Jung has a great deal to say about the necessary readjustments in the second half of life:

"We cannot live the afternoon of life according to the programme of life's morning—for what was great in the morning will be little at evening, and what in the morning was true will at evening have become a lie. . . . Ageing people should know that their lives are not mounting and unfolding, but that an inexorable inner process forces the contraction of life. For a young person it is almost a sin—and certainly a danger—to be too much occupied with himself; but for the ageing person it is a duty and a necessity to give serious attention to himself. After having lavished its light upon the world, the sun withdraws its rays in order to illumine itself. Instead of doing likewise, many old people prefer to be hypochondriacs, niggards, doctrinaires, applauders of the past or eternal adolescents—all lamentable substitutes for the illumination of the self, but inevitable consequences of the delusion that the second half of life must be governed by the principles of the first. . . . Whoever carries on into the afternoon the law of the morning—that is, the aims of nature—must pay for so doing with damage to his soul just as surely as a growing youth who tries to salvage his childish egoism must pay for his mistake with social failure. Money-making, social existence, family and posterity are nothing but plain nature—not culture. Culture lies beyond the purpose of nature. Could by any chance culture be the meaning and purpose of the second half of life?"

If we accept Jung's argument, Jaques is the one assuredly

sane and sensible person in the play. In relinquishing whatever may have been his former mode of life for a contemplative existence; in reinforcing this aim at the end of the play by a determination to apply himself to the tremendous problems of sin and redemption, Jaques is seeking self-illumination in a spiritual awareness that will come to the mature William Shakespeare, culminating at the peak of his philosophic, if not his dramatic, achievement: *The Tempest*.

Shakespeare was in his mid-thirties when he wrote *As You Like It*, still young by today's standards, but well into middle life by those of his time. His art could no longer be satisfied with gay comedy and swift-moving historical drama. He was to progress through more astringent comedy and deep tragedy to the ultimate "problem plays" of redemption and regeneration. Jaques has already made the alteration of aim which Jung requires of every man; finally Shakespeare leaves him in meditation in his hermit's cell, whence he resurrects him twelve years later in the guise of Prospero.

Most critics place *As You Like It* before *Twelfth Night* in the chronology of the plays; but where all is conjecture psychological evidence may be as valid as historical, and I prefer to accept *As You Like It* as the last of what Ivor Brown calls Shakespeare's "high fantastical" period.

Helen Gardner infers that Jaques arrogates to himself the divine role, quoting Francis Bacon: "In this theatre of man's life it is reserved only for God and angels to be lookers-on." Prospero has also been attacked by critics as a man who, by opting out of normal human existence, has taken to himself the powers of God in his island kingdom. I find nothing blasphemous in either. What was a spiritual spark in Jaques has become a flame in Prospero, but he knows that his power is not truly divine—because not eternal, just as Shakespeare's life could not be eternal.

Jaques is part of Shakespeare's genius and later preoccupation with the spiritual side of man's nature, a preoccupation proper to his own maturity and not a subject for reproach.

# 7

## HAMLET—THE MANIC-DEPRESSIVE

THE only defence that I can proffer to the charge of adding wantonly to the voluminous literature on *Hamlet* is that no treatise on Shakespeare's melancholics would be complete without at least a passing reference to this play. But I must go further, because a wide survey of the text is needed to fulfil my aim of drawing my inferences from Shakespeare's own words rather than from unsupported theory.

Although in general I accept the opinion of others before me who have decided that Hamlet is truly melancholic in both the Elizabethan and the modern connotation of the term, there are for me passages in the text which both extend and modify this assumption in ways that appear to have escaped the critics' notice. I have also formulated views on Hamlet's mental state at successive stages in the play which I believe to be original.

As always, Hamlet's opening speech poses and reveals the character. The Queen tells him:

> Thou know'st 'tis common: all that lives must die,
> Passing through nature to eternity.

The dialogue proceeds:

> HAMLET: Ay, madam, it is common.
> QUEEN:                            If it be,
> Why seems it so particular with thee?
> HAMLET: Seems, madam! Nay, it is: I know not "seems".
> 'Tis not alone my inky cloak, good mother,
> Nor customary suits of solemn black,
> Nor windy suspiration of forced breath,
> No, nor the fruitful river of the eye,
> Nor the dejected haviour of the visage,
> Together with all forms, moods, shapes of grief
> That can denote me truly. These indeed seem,

> For they are actions that a man might play;
> But I have that within which passes show:
> These but the trappings and the suits of woe.

The situation is not unfamiliar—the patient who is said not to have recovered from the shock of a personal bereavement, often years before, which is persistently brought up by him and his relatives to explain a condition which they cannot understand, parallel to the emphasis on Antonio's business worries. The climax of the speech, which appears to have eluded the critics, is the penultimate line. The sensation of something strange and oppressive welling up within the body is a diagnostic feature of psychotic melancholia.

This speech seems to call for a delivery in the flat monotone of the truly melancholic, and I have witnessed a rendering of this quality from Richard Burton. But dramatic needs will not tolerate a continuation of this approach to the character; variations of pitch and tempo cannot be withheld for long.

I need not quote the first soliloquy, when Hamlet is alone on the stage, stripped of any compulsion to restrain the outpouring of his sad thoughts. The suicidal tendency is self-explanatory, and we have the usual mechanism of projection and rationalization by which the patient accounts to himself for the cloud which hangs heavily upon him. In considering the vehemence of his condemnation of his mother it must be remembered that marriage to a deceased husband's brother was definitely accounted incestuous in Shakespeare's day.

At this stage the crux of the character problem is whether Hamlet has sufficient cause to drive a normal person to the point of suicidal despair. Freud says that it is no unusual thing for a man to develop a depressive illness with loss of working capacity after the death of his father; but, though not unusual, this depression cannot be regarded as a normal reaction. I agree with T. S. Eliot's opinion that Hamlet's emotion is in excess of the facts as they appear, and therefore not completely expressible.

There follows Hamlet's reunion with his friends, Marcellus and Horatio. Horatio is an important figure, because Hamlet trusts him implicitly, and their duologues reveal as much of the true Hamlet as the soliloquies.

In the next scene it appears that Laertes holds no great opinion of Hamlet's moral character. He harangues his sister at considerable length:

> For Hamlet, and the trifling of his favour,
> Hold it a fashion, and a toy in blood,
> A violet in the youth of primy nature,
> Forward, not permanent, sweet, not lasting,
> The perfume and suppliance of a minute:
> No more . . .
>                 . . . Perhaps he loves you now,
> And now no soil nor cautel doth besmirch
> The virtue of his will: but you must fear,
> His greatness weighed, his will is not his own;
> For he himself is subject to his birth.
> He may not, as unvalued persons do,
> Carve for himself, for on his choice depends
> The sanity and health of this whole state,
> And therefore must his choice be circumscribed
> Unto the voice and yielding of that body
> Whereof he is the head.

At some further length he warns her of the risk of yielding to Hamlet's importunity—later reinforced more pungently by Polonius:

> In few, Ophelia,
> Do not believe his vows; for they are brokers,
> Not of that dye which their investments show,
> But mere implorators of unholy suits,
> Breathing like sanctified and pious bawds,
> The better to beguile.

As in the case of Hamlet's melancholy, these arguments are in excess of the observed facts. Why should Ophelia not be a fit match for Hamlet, and why should those who might be expected to welcome it most damn the suggestion with such importunate emphasis? No other woman is mentioned in the play who might be a more politic choice for Hamlet. If Shakespeare had this point in mind why did he not produce a sister for Fortinbras, or some other person of royal blood? It cannot be suggested that the daughter of the principal Councillor of State  is too far below the throne to merit consideration. The history of the Tudor monarchy gives no grounds for the acceptance of this supposition by Shakespeare's audience.

Further, Polonius and Laertes have no textual support for their imputation to Hamlet of sexual promiscuity. To no one else in the play does he appear as other than an upright, moral, serious-minded young man, beloved by the people and by no means the sort to breed a reputation for imprudent dalliance.

Are we then to assume that both Polonius and Laertes are activated by the motive of sheer malice? Dr Johnson says that "the character of Polonius is solved by the idea of dotage encroaching on wisdom"—he has vast wisdom stored from the past, but cannot tackle new circumstances. His false appraisal of Hamlet may perhaps be part of his incipient dotage; but Laertes has no such excuse. He is presented to us as an honest and likeable young man, and it is only later in the play that his grief for the deaths of his father and sister converts him to pliant complicity in the designs of Claudius.

In my experience there is only one common reason for parents to object to the marriage of their daughter with an otherwise eligible young man—and that is a history of mental illness either in himself or in his family. In spite of Professor Sewell's warning not to adduce motives which do not appear in the text, I can understand the behaviour of Laertes and Polonius only by the assumption that Hamlet had shown signs of mental imbalance before the period of the play. To give Ophelia the true reason for their opposition might evoke her pity and strengthen her in a resolve not to be parted from Hamlet. Robert Speaight suggests that it was in fact true that Hamlet had made Ophelia his mistress: this would add force to the warning that he could never marry her and that his love was insincere. Perhaps, even so, a stronger character would not have withdrawn her love so readily, but Ophelia is only demonstrating a kind of weak suggestibility which is obviously a family failing.

Hamlet's encounter with his father's ghost on the battlements does not call for extended quotation. Critics are not in agreement whether the Ghost's story implies that Gertrude was unfaithful to him before his death or not. The relevant lines are these:

> Ay, that incestuous, that adulterate beast,
> With witchcraft of his wit, with traitorous gifts—
> O wicked wit and gifts, that have the power
> So to seduce!—won to his shameful lust
> The will of my most seeming-virtuous queen.

The incest and adultery may simply refer to the later marriage, and it is not necessary to assume that Gertrude was guilty of any overt sexual misconduct before her husband's death. If this were so, Hamlet's bitterness against his mother would be more pointed, but I would still consider it in excess of normal.

The main relevance of the Ghost to Hamlet's mental condition is in the consideration whether it is an "honest" ghost or a creation of his own mind—an hallucination. Shakespeare himself may not have believed in ghosts, but he was writing for an audience that did; it is also perfectly clear that the Ghost is seen by Horatio, Marcellus and the other guards on watch. But though there is no suggestion of a visual hallucination, the Ghost speaks only to Hamlet. Dr Somerville judges that Hamlet is hallucinated both in the swearing from the "cellarage" and later at the reappearance of the Ghost in Gertrude's bedchamber; but I agree with Bradley that this is not so. It is a dramatic convention that a character may be heard clearly by the audience and by only one other person on the stage, and it is not remarkable that Horatio and Marcellus should not be tuned to the Ghost's objurgations beneath them.

In the later scene it must be remembered that the Ghost has bidden Hamlet:

> nor let thy soul contrive
> Against thy mother aught. Leave her to heaven,
> And to those thorns that in her bosom lodge
> To prick and sting her.

This is also the ghost of the man:

> So loving to my mother
> That he might not beteem the winds of heaven
> Visit her face too roughly.

What is more natural than that he should have a particular care not to alarm Gertrude by making his ghostly presence visible and audible to her as well as to Hamlet?

But the proof of the Ghost's "honesty" is to be given later, not by the trick played on Claudius by Hamlet, but in a speech which Hamlet does not overhear. It is necessary to emphasize the importance of this issue, because, if it is accepted that Hamlet is hallucinated, he cannot be suffering from a simple depressive illness. Hallucinations are characteristic of toxic brain conditions and particularly of schizophrenia; they never appear in the manic-depressive psychosis.

After his first encounter with the Ghost Hamlet proceeds to make the critic's task more difficult by adjuring his friends:

> How strange or odd some'er I bear myself,
> As I perchance hereafter shall think meet
> To put an antic disposition on—

to swear that they will not reveal the cause of this.

It is difficult to understand what Hamlet has to gain by feigning insanity; it certainly does not help him to make more certain of the guilt of Claudius, nor to carry out his revenge. The answer may possibly be found in the savage penalties exacted for plotting against the head of the state in Shakespeare's day. Those who have read a detailed account of the fate which befell the members of the Babington and Guy Fawkes conspiracies will realize that, even to a melancholic, such a means of indirect suicide would have little appeal. By establishing to the Court that he is not responsible for his actions, Hamlet can, and indeed does, avoid the fate of a criminal when his plans miscarry. The assumed insanity is put on mainly for the benefit of Polonius, whose wagging tongue can be relied on to spread the news throughout the Court.

To decide at what moment the "antic disposition" takes over is more difficult. Harry Levin makes the distinction that between Hamlet's verse and prose passages. He considers that all the verse is sincere, with which I agree; but I find Hamlet often at his wittiest and most logical in the prose sequences. To be effective dramatically the assumed insanity must be obvious, as in the baiting of Polonius. Where there is doubt, I reject it, and consider most of the irrationality as part of the character.

At the beginning of Act II Ophelia describes to Polonius her encounter with Hamlet, fresh from his conversation with the Ghost:

> My lord, as I was sewing in my closet,
> Lord Hamlet, with his doublet all unbraced,
> No hat upon his head, his stockings fouled,
> Ungartered and down-gyved to his ankle,
> Pale as his shirt, his knees knocking each other;
> And with a look so piteous in purport
> As if he had been loosed out of hell
> To speak of horrors, he comes before me.
> . . . . . . . . . . . . . . . . . . . . . . . . . .
> He took me by the wrist and held me hard;
> Then goes he to the length of all his arm,
> And with his other hand thus o'er his brow,

He falls to such perusal of my face
As a would draw it. Long stayed he so.
At last, a little shaking of mine arm,
And thrice his head thus waving up and down,
He raised a sigh so piteous and profound
As it did seem to shatter all his bulk
And end his being. That done, he lets me go,
And with his head over his shoulder turned,
He seemed to find his way without his eyes;
For out o'doors he went without their help
And to the last bended their light on me.

This is clearly real and not assumed distraction. Dover Wilson points out the effect it would have on Hamlet when Ophelia, who has already denied him access at her father's bidding, produces no word of comfort for him in his pitiable condition. He accounts thus for Hamlet's virulence in the "nunnery" scene, which I will consider in due course.

Polonius is satisfied that Hamlet's distraught condition stems from his rejected love for Ophelia, a view which Hamlet is happy to encourage by writing to her nonsensical verse:

Doubt that the stars are fire;
Doubt that the sun doth move;
Doubt truth to be a liar;
But never doubt I love.

This is a type of doggerel essentially different from Hamlet's outburst after the success of the "play" scene, and one which could never come from his scholarly mind uncontrived. The "antic disposition" has made its first appearance.

Hamlet reinforces his effect in his next conversation with Polonius; yet, as the latter notes, "there is method in't", whereby his apparently inconsequential sentences conceal barbs directed at his adversary. But the genuine melancholy is not far below the surface. When Polonius asks if he will walk out of the air, Hamlet's reply: "Into my grave" inspires in the old gentleman an unusually profound observation:

How pregnant some of his replies are! A happiness that often madness hits on, which reason and sanity could not so prosperously be delivered of (i.e. the unconscious mind takes over).

In the meantime, Claudius has adopted a device much in

favour with the relatives of sick persons today—he has summoned Hamlet's friends, Rosencrantz and Guildenstern, to spy on him and report on the cause and manifestations of his disorder, evidently with strict injunctions not to divulge that they have been sent for specially for this purpose. But like all melancholics, Hamlet retains the intellectual acuity to see through so transparent a device. His dialogue with Rosencrantz and Guildenstern is fanciful, but bears no trace of assumed insanity; it conveys to the audience, as well as to his friends, the true stamp of his melancholy:

> HAMLET: What have you, my good friends, deserved at the hands of fortune that she sends you to prison hither?
> GUILDENSTERN: Prison, my lord?
> HAMLET: Denmark's a prison.
> ROSENCRANTZ: Then is the world one.
> HAMLET: A goodly one, in which there are many confines, wards and dungeons, Denmark being one o' th' worst.
> ROSENCRANTZ: We think not so, my lord.
> HAMLET: Why, then 'tis none to you; for there is nothing either good or bad but thinking makes it so. To me it is a prison.
> ROSENCRANTZ: Why, then your ambition makes it one: 'tis too narrow for your mind.
> HAMLET: O God, I could be bounded in a nutshell and count myself a king of infinite space, were it not that I have bad dreams.
> GUILDENSTERN: Which dreams indeed are ambition; for the very substance of the ambitious is merely the shadow of a dream.
> HAMLET: A dream itself is but a shadow.
> ROSENCRANTZ: Truly, and I hold ambition of so airy and light a quality that it is but a shadow's shadow.
> HAMLET: Then are our beggars bodies, and our monarchs and outstretched heroes the beggars' shadows. Shall we to the court? for, by my fay, I cannot reason.

After extracting Guildenstern's admission that they were sent for by Claudius, Hamlet himself gives them the reason for this:

> I have of late—but wherefore I know not—lost all my mirth, forgone all custom of exercises; and indeed it goes so heavily with my disposition that this goodly frame, the earth, seems to me a sterile promontory; this most excellent canopy, the air, look you, this brave o'erhanging firma-

ment, this majestical roof fretted with golden fire, why it
appeareth nothing to me but a foul and pestilent congrega-
tion of vapours. What a piece of work is a man! how noble
in reason! how infinite in faculties! in form and moving
how express and admirable! in action how like an angel!
in apprehension how like a god! the beauty of the world!
the paragon of animals! And yet, to me, what is this
quintessence of dust? Man delights not me, nor woman
neither, though by your smiling you seem to say so.

Kenneth Muir finds particularly in Hamlet's own description
of his melancholy in these passages a correspondence of the
symptoms with those given by Dr Timothy Bright in his treatise
on Melancholy, published in 1586, anticipating Robert Burton
by nearly forty years. Bright mentions the importance of exercise in treatment, using Hamlet's own words—"custom of
exercises". He shows how "the melancholy man ponders and
debates long, but when he acts moves vigorously". He says
that unnatural melancholy "raiseth the greatest tempest of
perturbation and most of all destroyeth the brain with all his
faculties and disposition of action". With melancholy men desperate fury is sometimes joined with fear, "which terrifieth, that
to avoid the terror they attempt sometimes to deprive themselves
of life, so irksome is it unto them through the tragical conceits;
although, weighing and considering death itself without comparison with force of the passion, some more fear of it than
they." . . . "The melancholy man is dull of deed, with a reasonably good memory if fancies deface it not . . . firm in opinion
and hardly removed where it is resolved: doubtful before, and
long in deliberation, suspicious—given to fearful and terrible
dreams; in affection sad, and full of fear." Finally: "the whole
force of the spirit . . . being close up in the dungeon of
melancholy darkness, imagineth all dark, black and full of
fear."

Professor Muir's masterstroke is the explanation of Hamlet's
madness "but north-north-west" from Bright's opinion that
"The air for melancholic folk ought to be thin, pure and subtle,
open and patent to all winds, in respect of their temper especially
to the south and south-east." The critics have argued for years
about the precise meaning of the word "handsaw" in this
passage, but have missed the far more important implication of
the wind direction.

In spite of this correspondence of terms and imagery, I am not convinced that Shakespeare read Timothy Bright's treatise himself. As I have already shown, there is equally good evidence that he read the *Anatomy of Melancholy*, published after his death. But this does not greatly matter. The important point is that Shakespeare's portrayal of melancholy in *Hamlet* corresponds closely with the description given by learned writers of his day; not only this—the symptoms hold equally good in any period as characteristic of a true psychotic depression.

Whatever our view of the moral character of Claudius, his management of the case of melancholia which he finds on his hands shows some commonsense, in spite of his failure to beguile the patient with the company of his old friends. Can we doubt that the arrival of the strolling players is another device of the King's to divert Hamlet with some amusement of a type which he appreciated in happier times?

I need not recount the genesis of the trap by which Hamlet turns the tables on Claudius; but his continued doubts of the Ghost's honesty are important:

> The spirit that I have seen
> May be a devil; and the devil hath power
> T'assume a pleasing shape; yea, and perhaps
> Out of my weakness and my melancholy
> Abuses me to damn me. I'll have grounds
> More relative than this. The play's the thing
> Wherein I'll catch the conscience of the King.

This shows that Hamlet has sufficient insight to be uncertain himself whether the Ghost may not be a projection of his own disordered mind. This is implicit in his idea that it might be the devil taking advantage of his melancholia to damn him. Lawrence Babb says that the devil's practice of victimizing melancholy men was common talk in Elizabethan times, so that this remaining doubt is a natural cause of Hamlet's restraint from immediate action.

Meanwhile, not satisfied with the report of Rosencrantz and Guildenstern, the King arranges to eavesdrop with Polonius on a prearranged meeting between Hamlet and Ophelia, which leads to the famous "nunnery" scene. Here, a chance remark from Polonius extracts an "aside" which gives the first hint of Claudius's guilty conscience:

POLONIUS:                We are oft to blame in this—
'Tis too much proved—that with devotion's visage
And pious action do we sugar o'er
The devil himself.

CLAUDIUS:              O, 'tis too true!
How smart a lash that speech doth give my conscience!
The harlot's cheek, beautied with plast'ring art,
Is not more ugly to the thing that helps it
Than is my deed to my most painted word.
O heavy burthen!

I will not quote the soliloquy beginning "To be, or not to be"; it is sufficient for my purpose to remark that Hamlet is again contemplating suicide. His change of mood at the end is one of Shakespeare's happiest inspirations:

> Soft you now!
> The fair Ophelia! Nymph, in thy orisons
> Be all my sins remembered.

The pathos engendered is similar to that derived from Othello's:

> Soft you: a word or two before you go.

Surely this heart-rending appeal cannot be sarcastic. If not, then it cannot be doubted that Hamlet's love for Ophelia is genuine and that its renunciation is reluctant and grievous.

It has been suggested that, psychologically, Hamlet cannot commit murder until he has cast out love, but I do not postulate any complicated symbolism in this scene. It is Ophelia who aggravates her rejection of Hamlet by returning his presents. The changes in Hamlet's mood from this point are so important that I must quote extensively before discussion:

OPHELIA:  My lord, I have remembrances of yours
That I have longed long to redeliver.
I pray you now receive them.

HAMLET:               No, not I.
I never gave you aught.

OPHELIA:  My honoured lord, you know right well you did;
And with them words of so sweet breath composed
As made the things more rich. Their perfume lost,
Take these again; for to the noble mind
Rich gifts wax poor when givers prove unkind.
There, my lord.

HAMLET:   Ha, ha! Are you honest?

OPHELIA:  My lord?

HAMLET:   Are you fair?

OPHELIA:  What means your lordship?

HAMLET:   That if you be honest and fair, your honesty
should admit no discourse to your beauty.

OPHELIA:  Could beauty, my lord, have better commerce
than with honesty?

HAMLET:   Ay, truly; for the power of beauty will sooner
transform honesty from what it is to a bawd than
the force of honesty can translate beauty into his
likeness. This was sometime a paradox, but now
the time gives it proof. I did love you once.

OPHELIA:  Indeed, my lord, you made me believe so.

HAMLET:   You should not have believed me; for virtue
cannot so inoculate our old stock but we shall
relish of it. I loved you not.

OPHELIA:  I was the more deceived.

HAMLET:   Get thee to a nunnery. Why wouldst thou be a
breeder of sinners? I am myself indifferent
honest, but yet I could accuse me of such things
that it were better my mother had not borne me.
I am very proud, revengeful, ambitious; with
more offences at my beck than I have thoughts
to put them in, imagination to give them shape,
or time to act them in. What should such fellows
as I do crawling between earth and heaven? We
are arrant knaves all: believe none of us. Go thy
ways to a nunnery. Where's your father?

OPHELIA:  At home, my lord.

HAMLET:   Let the doors be shut upon him, that he may play
the fool nowhere but in's own house. Farewell.

OPHELIA:  O, help him, you sweet heavens!

HAMLET:   If thou dost marry, I'll give thee this plague for
thy dowry: Be thou as chaste as ice, as pure as
snow, thou shalt not escape calumny. Get thee
to a nunnery, go. Farewell. Or, if thou wilt needs
marry, marry a fool, for wise men know well
enough what monsters you make of them. To a
nunnery, go; and quickly too. Farewell.

OPHELIA:  O heavenly powers restore him!

HAMLET:   I have heard of your paintings too, well enough:
God hath given you one face, and you make
yourselves another. You jig and amble, and you
lisp, and nickname God's creatures, and make

> your wantonness your ignorance. Go to, I'll no
> more on't: it hath made me mad. I say, we will
> have no more marriages. Those that are married
> already, all but one, shall live; the rest shall keep
> as they are. To a nunnery, go.

This scene has often tripped up those critics who have rele-
gated the play from the theatre to the study, leading them to
suggest that Hamlet's "Ha, ha! Are you honest?" comes from
his observation of a movement behind the arras. Harry Levin
indicates a break at this point because Hamlet changes to prose.
In fact, Hamlet's few words to Ophelia after the soliloquy are
metrically ambiguous, and Ophelia's startled "My lord!" is the
first phrase that is definitely prose. The movement behind the
arras is a clumsy device, very difficult to time convincingly in
production, and I agree with Dover Wilson that Hamlet has
overheard the plot at an earlier stage. He is conscious all the
time of the conspirators behind the arras, but is at first uncertain
of Ophelia's complicity. Dramatically and psychologically,
Hamlet is uncommitted until Ophelia has not only returned his
gifts but wounded him further by accusing him of unkindness,
for which there is no justification in the text. His "Ha, ha!" is an
expression of grief, not of surprise. But he will not accuse her
without further testing. If she is honest she will surely be moved
by the abjectness of his self-accusatory catalogue. The enumera-
tion of his faults is characteristic of the sense of unworthiness of
the true melancholic, and I regard it as absolutely sincere.
Freud considers that the melancholic, in decrying himself, is
nearer to the truth than in his normal self-sufficient pride,
quoting Hamlet as an example.

It will be noted that, up to this point, Hamlet's bitterness has
been directed against the world and against himself—his attitude to Ophelia has been one of agonized appeal, not of reproach. When she fails to respond, he asks a direct question:
"Where is your father?" She answers this with a direct lie, and
Hamlet, by a study of her face, knows that this is so. The rest of
his lines are directed, partly to Ophelia, partly to the hidden
listeners, and come partly from the heart. Dramatically the
gain in effect of a break of mood at "Where's your father?"
is unmistakable, and I am sure that this was the author's
intention.

It has not, I think, been noted that the King overhears in

"those that are married, all but one, shall live" a definite warning that Hamlet has designs on his life, which is of some importance in considering his reaction to the "Mousetrap".

After Hamlet's exit. Ophelia sheds some light on his general repute:

> O, what a noble mind is here o'erthrown!
> The courtier's, soldier's, scholar's eye, tongue, sword;
> Th'expectancy and rose of the fair state,
> The glass of fashion and the world of form,
> Th' observed of all observers, quite, quite down!

This does not sound like the nasty libertine she ought to believe him if she is right in obeying her father's injunctions. But it is too late now for tender speeches. If only she had shown her pity to Hamlet himself, instead of returning his presents with such brutal tactlessness! Her fumbling ineptitude at this point is one of the mainsprings of the tragedy.

Claudius is now sceptical of love for Ophelia as the reason for Hamlet's madness:

> Love! his affections do not that way tend;
> Nor what he spake, though it lacked form a little,
> Was not like madness. There's something in his soul
> O'er which his melancholy sits on brood,
> And I do doubt the hatch and the disclose
> Will be some danger; which for to prevent,
> I have in quick determination
> Thus set it down:—He shall with speed to England,
> For the demand of our neglected tribute.
> Haply the seas and countries different
> With variable objects shall expel
> This something-settled matter in his heart,
> Whereon his brains still beating puts him thus
> From fashion of himself.

The King is not so easily deceived as Polonius. He knows a hawk from a handsaw, showing both a shrewd appreciation of the causes of melancholy and a sound knowledge of treatment accepted throughout the ages. The patient is to be sent on a long voyage, whereby the sea air and change of scene may combine to effect a recovery.

Hamlet's attack on Ophelia, when ostensibly alone with her, is abusive, but not vulgar. At the start of the play scene he indulges in the following, in the full presence of the Court:

HAMLET: Lady, shall I lie in your lap?
OPHELIA: No, my lord.
HAMLET: I mean, my head upon your lap?
OPHELIA: Ay, my lord.
HAMLET: Do you think I meant country matters?
OPHELIA: I think nothing, my lord.
HAMLET: That's a fair thought to lie between maids' legs.
OPHELIA: What is, my lord?
HAMLET: Nothing.

This brutal coarseness is something new, as if the veneer of civilized courtesy had been stripped from Hamlet, which is precisely what happens in the milder degrees of mania.

The stage directions for the dumb-show that follows are these:

Enter a King and a Queen very lovingly; the Queen embracing him, and he her. She kneels and makes show of protestation unto him. He takes her up, and declines his head upon her neck. He lays him down upon a bank of flowers. She, seeing him asleep, leaves him. Anon comes in another man, takes off his crown and kisses it, pours poison in the sleeper's ears and leaves him. The Queen returns, finds the King dead, makes passionate action. The Poisoner, with some three or four, comes in again, seems to condole with her. The dead body is carried away. The Poisoner woos the Queen with gifts: she seems harsh awhile, but in the end accepts his love.

No wonder that Hamlet complains: "the players cannot keep counsel; they'll tell all." The murder, as described by the Ghost, has been completely re-enacted, springing the trap prematurely. But the King has not moved a muscle! The critics have given diverse explanations for this: that he was not paying attention; that he was keeping himself under control; that the Ghost's story was untrue and therefore meaningless to him. I think that Claudius would be more interested in Hamlet than in the players, and might well give only cursory glances at the dumb-show. Dramatically, the visual imagination is not so strong as the auditory; a mimed play without words, seen on a television screen, is less effective than a sound broadcast without vision.

The eyes only see what they are directed upon, whereas the ears absorb sound from every quarter.

Apart from what might be a routine inquiry about any possible offence in the play the King remains silent until the actual poisoning. Considering that Claudius has overheard Hamlet's veiled threat in the "nunnery" scene, it is interesting that the poisoner in *The Mousetrap* is "one Lucianus, nephew to the King". It has been suggested by Dover Wilson that fear for his own life rather than a guilty conscience causes Claudius to rise in alarm.

Fortunately, all these arguments come to be settled in the next scene. In his only long soliloquy Claudius admits his crime without expressing any specific fear of Hamlet, and it is quite clear that his conscience has been aroused by *The Mousetrap*, proving effectually that the Ghost's story is true.

Left alone with Horatio, Hamlet breaks out into doggerel verse:

> Why let the strucken deer go weep,
> The hart ungalled play;
> For some must watch, while some must sleep:
> Thus runs the world away.
> Would not this, sir, and a forest of feathers—if the rest of my fortunes turn Turk with me—with two Provincial roses on my razed shoes, get me a fellowship in a cry of players, sir?
> . . . . . . . . . . . . . . . . . . . . . . . . . . . . . . . . . . .
> > For thou dost know, O Damon dear,
> > This realm dismantled was
> > Of Jove himself; and now reigns here
> > A very, very—pajock.

This is not assumed insanity; Hamlet has nothing to conceal from his friend Horatio. But the levity and incomplete coherence are in excess of the normal effects of triumph on the successful conclusion of his plot. The lines are not completely senseless, but there is a compression of ideas and imagery, which are further characteristics of psychotic mania. I regard this passage as incontrovertible evidence of Hamlet's genuinely elated state, and accept the later tasteless levity with the body of Polonius as uncontrollable and not assumed.

Note the contrast in the following:

HAMLET: Do you see yonder cloud that's almost in shape of
   a camel?

POLONIUS: By the mass, and 'tis like a camel indeed.
HAMLET: Methinks it is like a weasel.
POLONIUS: It is backed like a weasel.
HAMLET: Or like a whale.
POLONIUS: Very like a whale.

Here we have Hamlet's "antic disposition", with Polonius humouring the "madman"—and there is no doubt about it.

Hamlet's failure to kill Claudius when he comes upon him at his prayers has excited much comment. I see nothing irresolute in this. In Elizabethan times, when life on earth was constantly at hazard, the life hereafter assumed a greater significance. Thus I find it easy to accept Hamlet's own explanation that his revenge would be incomplete if the newly shriven soul should thereby attain immortal bliss.

Whatever her husband's view, the Queen is satisfied that Hamlet's madness is dangerous. After some acrimonious exchanges, Hamlet bids her:

Come, come, and sit you down. You shall not budge.
You go not till I set you up a glass
Where you may see the inmost part of you.

Although Hamlet's tone is bullying, he makes no threat of physical violence; yet Gertrude exclaims:

What wilt thou do? Thou wilt not murder me?
Help, help, ho!

Perhaps there is something of his pathological elation in Hamlet's eyes. Certainly his wild pass through the arras is quite at variance with all his former scruples. He delays his revenge until satisfied beyond a doubt of the Ghost's honesty, but has no hesitation in striking blindly at an unseen eavesdropper, in the full knowledge that Claudius had Polonius with him on a parallel occasion. Whatever may be attributed to the heat of the moment, Hamlet's action is here beyond the bounds of any definition of sanity. Equally irrational is the immediate resumption of his lecture to his mother after a curt dismissal from his thoughts of the horribly dead Polonius.

Robert Speaight describes this scene as the emotional, but not the dramatic, climax of the play. Once Hamlet has begun the outpouring of his pent-up emotion he cannot cease until the catharsis is complete. Midway, his father's ghost reappears to issue a salutary reminder that his immediate duty is the despatch of Claudius. Wiser than Hamlet, his father knows that Gertrude is incapable of self-criticism; and the achievement of this long and passionate harangue is, in fact, negligible. At no point does Gertrude show any true penetration of her emotional reserve. Hamlet's appeal to her to absent herself from the King's bed goes unanswered, drawing from him this sarcastic threat:

> Let the bloat King tempt you again to bed;
> Pinch wanton on your cheek, call you his mouse;
> And let him for a pair of reechy kisses,
> Or paddling in your neck with his damned fingers,
> Make you to ravel all this matter out,
> That I essentially am not in madness,
> But mad in craft. 'Twere good you let him know;
> For who, that's but a queen, fair, sober, wise,
> Would from a paddock, from a bat, a gib,
> Such dear concernings hide? Who would do so?
> No, in despite of sense and secrecy,
> Unpeg the basket on the house's top,
> Let the birds fly, and like the famous ape,
> To try conclusions, in the basket creep
> And break your own neck down.

The fable is lost, but the sense of it is that if the Queen betrays his secret it will bring about her downfall. Her reply is feeble and obviously insincere:

> Be thou assured, if words be made of breath
> And breath of life, I have no life to breathe
> What thou hast said to me.

Hamlet's concern to preserve his cloak of insanity after the death of Polonius strengthens my conviction that the reason for it is to escape the consequences of such an action as has in fact occurred. This injunction to his mother leads him to the practical issue which confronts all murderers—the disposal of the body:

> I'll lug the guts into the neighbour room.
> Mother, good night indeed. This counsellor
> Is now most still, most secret and most grave,
> Who was in life a foolish prating knave.
> Come, sir, to draw towards an end with you.
> Good night, mother.

After an undignified chase round the castle, Hamlet is apprehended and brought to the King; this dialogue ensues:

KING: Now, Hamlet, where's Polonius?

HAMLET: At supper.

KING: At supper! Where?

HAMLET: Not where he eats, but where he is eaten. A certain convocation of politic worms are e'en at him. Your worm is your only emperor for diet. We fat all creatures else to fat us, and we fat ourselves for maggots. Your fat king and your lean beggar is but variable service, two dishes, but to one table. That's the end.

KING: Alas, alas!

HAMLET: A man may fish with the worm that hath eat of a king, and eat of the fish that hath fed of that worm.

KING: What dost thou mean by this?

HAMLET: Nothing but to show you how a king may go a progress through the guts of a beggar.

KING: Where is Polonius?

HAMLET: In heaven: send thither to see. If your messenger find him not there, seek him i' th' other place yourself. But if, indeed, you find him not within this month, you shall nose him as you go up the stairs into the lobby.

KING: Go seek him there.

HAMLET: He will stay till you come.

As Claudius has remarked earlier, this, though it lacks form a little, is not like madness, and would never deceive so shrewd a psychologist as Claudius. The general content is sensible and witty; it is only the context which is wrong.

This is a convenient point to consider the "madness" of Hamlet generally. The critics argue as if sanity and madness were recognizable concrete opposites, whereas there are innumerable qualifying factors according to the purpose for which a definition is required. That given by Polonius is the most absurd. If true madness is to be nothing else but mad then the majority of certified madmen are sane. Hamlet, whether mad or not, certainly comprehends in his character almost more other things than can be dreamed of in our philosophy.

I should like to approach the question of Hamlet's sanity by posing three questions—applicable to mental illness in this country today:

1. Is Hamlet insane from a legal point of view: that is, does he suffer from a defect of reason whereby, in the murder of Polonius, he does not appreciate the nature or the quality

of the act, or, alternatively, does he not know that it is wrong?

In the *Oresteia*, with which *Hamlet* has many links, Orestes is placed in a seemingly insoluble dilemma. Filial piety demands that he should wreak vengeance on his father's murderers, which include his mother; if he fails, his father's spirit will loose the Furies on him. But matricide is wrong, and if he succeeds, his mother's spirit will treat him in the same way.

The Ghost has enjoined Hamlet to murder Claudius, and we have accepted the Ghost's "honesty". Does this mean that this murder is morally right? And, if so, is the accidental killing of Polonius in the pursuit of this objective also blameless? I do not see why we should take a view on this issue different from modern conceptions of morality. In Shakespeare's day, regicide, for good or bad reasons, was common; but I do not think that it was accepted as morally justifiable. Hamlet's duty is to bring the King to judgement. A reasonable and sagacious prince in Shakespeare's day would not have attacked this objective by the direct means of his own sword, but would have gathered supporters round him with a *coup d'état* as their goal.

Since the inception of the M'Naughton Rules, judges have maintained a cautious and conservative view of criminal irresponsibility. To them, the fact that a murderer has taken steps to cover his tracks has sufficed to show that he knew that his actions were wrong. But the medical profession hold it possible that a man may attempt to evade the legal consequences of what he has done without necessarily believing it to be morally blameworthy.

Fortunately, the recently established doctrine of diminished responsibility brings the two points of view closer together—and provides a basis for dealing with Hamlet. By reason of the disordered state of his emotions he is not fully responsible for his actions, and would today be found guilty of the reduced charge of manslaughter.

The second question I pose is this:

2. Is Hamlet deluded? i.e. has he a belief in something that a

normal person of his time would not accept as true? Again accepting the Ghost as "honest", the answer must be "no".

Finally:

3. Is he certifiable? By this I mean to inquire whether, in his own interests or for the protection of society, he should be placed under restraint.

By the recent Mental Health Act this problem is greatly simplified. The certifying doctor has merely to describe the clinical picture and explain briefly why voluntary treatment is inappropriate. But, prior to November 1960, certification by a Justice of the Peace on medical advice involved a problem of the same degree as that faced by a medical author in giving a similar opinion to the reading public: the doctor had to adduce evidence of abnormal behaviour such as would be accepted by an ordinary member of society with no medical knowledge.

The first section of the certificate was headed: "Facts observed by myself." In Hamlet's case we may conveniently consider the physician as an eavesdropper during his dissertation on the corpse of Polonius. As I have suggested, this cannot be assumed insanity, both because the content is too sensible and also because such macabre detachment after such an appalling deed would surely be beyond the simulation even of an intelligence as alert as Hamlet's.

To explain briefly why this conversation indicates unsoundness of mind is not easy. As I said before, it is a matter of context. The progress of a king through the guts of a beggar is a witty and scholarly conception, suitable for the court dinner table, but not for the circumstances in which Hamlet meets Claudius after the death of Polonius. The modern equivalent of the parable is the song *On Ilkla Moor Baht 'At*. To sing this in a public house or even in the bath need not excite remark—but at an official function it could be instanced as evidence of unsoundness of mind.

The second section of the certificate: "Facts communicated to me by others", is more difficult. The chief witness, Polonius himself, is dead; Horatio is sworn to silence, and Rosencrantz and Guildenstern are not very reliable. The Queen's account of the murder of Polonius, with Hamlet's subsequent verbal assault, must serve to show that his present mood is abnormal and physically dangerous.

I am satisfied that, using the procedures either prior or subsequent to the new Mental Health Act, Hamlet is at this point certifiable in a medical sense. Here we have the apparent paradox which has caused the critics to take such divergent views of his sanity. He has no delusions, and is therefore not insane according to the popular conception of the term; a court of law would find him partly responsible for his actions; but a medical practitioner would have no difficulty in certifying that he should be deprived of his liberty for the protection of others.

Hamlet has one soliloquy before his departure for England. In this he seems to be back in his depressed self-accusatory mood, comparing the vast military preparations of Fortinbras for the conquest of a few barren acres of Polish soil with his own inaction in face of a matter of deep personal honour:

> How all occasions do inform against me,
> And spur my dull revenge! What is a man,
> If his chief good and market of his time
> Be but to sleep and feed? A beast, no more.
> Sure, he that made us with such large discourse,
> Looking before and after, gave us not
> That capability and godlike reason
> To fust in us unused. Now, whether it be
> Bestial oblivion, ör some craven scruple
> Of thinking too precisely on th' event,—
> A thought which, quartered, hath but one part wisdom
> And every three parts coward—I do not know
> Why yet I live to say "This thing's to do,"
> Sith I have cause, and will, and strength, and means,
> To do't. . . .

This accusation of himself is not reasonable. Whatever justification Hamlet may have had for regarding his earlier delay as culpable, his fault now is that through too precipitate action he has killed the wrong man and alerted the King to his danger. He cannot now move unshadowed by Rosencrantz and Guildenstern, who are ready to anticipate any further violent impulse on his part.

The concluding phrase of the soliloquy:

> From this time forth
> My thoughts be bloody, or be nothing worth!

is uncharacteristic of Hamlet, and the speech is so often omitted that there is some justification for those who fall into the common error of attributing it to Macbeth. But I think that Shakespeare had a special purpose here, to prepare us for Hamlet's apparently callous treatment of Rosencrantz and Guildenstern. It is explained by Harry Levin that this part of the plot is taken from the original legends which form the basis of *Hamlet*, and in which they had never been his close personal friends. But Shakespeare would not falsify a character to accommodate it to a pre-existing plot; and I think that we are to understand by this soliloquy that Hamlet is so full of self-reproach for his former scruples that any bloody action must be right for him now if it advances his main purpose.

Hamlet now departs on his voyage, and the remainder of Act IV is devoted mainly to the madness and death of Ophelia, which are not relevant to my purpose.

On Hamlet's return, in Act V, Shakespeare poses his character afresh in his first sentence:

> Has this fellow no feeling of his business that he sings in grave-making?

The last time we saw Hamlet he had been jesting coarsely about the body of the old man whom he had just murdered, and now his first utterance is to reprove the gravedigger for the venial fault of singing at his grim work! Surely this Hamlet must be marvellously changed.

In the ensuing dialogue the essential wit is that of the old Hamlet, but the philosophy is genuine and in accord with the circumstances. There is a remarkable parallelism in the imagery of the "noble dust of Alexander" and of the worms eating Polonius:

> Alexander died, Alexander was buried, Alexander returneth to dust; the dust is earth; of earth we make loam; and why of that loam, whereto he was converted, might not they stop a beer barrel?

Once more Hamlet breaks into doggerel verse:

> Imperious Caesar, dead and turned to clay,
> Might stop a hole to keep the wind away.

> O that that earth, which kept the world in awe,
> Should patch a wall t'expel the winter's flaw.

Compare this verse with that in Act III. It is no better as verse, but it has form and cohesion, and the thought content is consecutive. I am convinced that the returned Hamlet has recovered his wits and that the main purpose of the scene in the graveyard is to demonstrate this.

From the lips of Laertes, described by Hamlet as "a very noble youth", he learns for the first time of Ophelia's death. Laertes is unrestrained in his grief:

> O, treble woe
> Fall ten times treble on that curséd head
> Whose wicked deed thy most ingenious sense
> Deprived thee of! Hold off the earth awhile,
> Till I have caught her once more in my arms.
> Now pile your dust upon the quick and dead,
> Till of this flat a mountain you have made
> T'o'ertop old Pelion or the skyish head
> Of blue Olympus.

We may agree with Hamlet that this

> Phrase of sorrow
> Conjures the wandering stars and makes them stand
> Like wonder-wounded hearers . . .,

and his own riposte is merely competitive hyperbole:

> I loved Ophelia. Forty thousand brothers
> Could not, with all their quantity of love,
> Make up my sum. What wilt thou do for her?
> . . . . . . . . . . . . . . . . . . . . . . . .
> Woo't weep? woo't fight? woo't fast? woo't tear thyself?
> Woo't drink up eisel? eat a crocodile?
> I'll do't. Dost thou come here to whine?
> To outface me with leaping in her grave?
> Be buried quick with her, and so will I.
> And if thou prate of mountains, let them throw
> Millions of acres on us, till our ground,
> Singeing his pate against the burning zone,
> Make Ossa like a wart! Nay, and thou'lt mouth,
> I'll rant as well as thou.

Granted that Hamlet really did love Ophelia, the emotion here is not in excess of the cause, particularly from the shock of hearing of her death only at her funeral. Ernest Jones describes Hamlet's outburst as an over-compensation for his bad conscience, knowing that he was largely responsible for her death. This may be so, but I still regard this incident as psychologically normal, just as it appears so dramatically. Hamlet's attitude could be matched by the hero of any drama of the time without his mental stability being impugned at all. Curiously enough, this is one of the two points at which Robert Speaight concedes that Hamlet is genuinely mad—the other being at his murder of Polonius.

In the succeeding scene Hamlet shows the first sign of real insight and sensible planning for the solution of his problem. Again he is alone with Horatio:

> Sir, in my heart there was a kind of fighting
> That would not let me sleep. Methought I lay
> Worse than the mutines in the bilboes. Rashly,—
> And praised be rashness for it: let us know,
> Our indiscretion sometimes serves us well
> When our deep plots do pall; and that should learn us
> There's a divinity that shapes our ends,
> Rough-hew them how we will.

The final couplet is one of the well-known "quotations" in the play, but the opening lines are psychologically more important. What more succinct account of an acute mental disturbance could occupy a line and a half? The "rashness" which Hamlet praises is the burning of his boats by the despatch of Rosencrantz and Guildenstern; this he is prepared to justify:

> Why, man, they did make love to their employment,
> They are not on my conscience: their defeat
> Does by their own insinuation grow.
> 'Tis dangerous when the baser nature comes
> Between the pass and fell incensed points
> Of mighty opposites.

Now, for the first time, Hamlet puts the offences of Claudius into proper proportion:

> He that hath killed my king and whored my mother;
> Popped in between th' election and my hopes;
> Thrown out his angle for my proper life,
> And with such coz'nage—is't not perfect conscience,
> To quit him with this arm? And is't not to be damned,

7

To let this canker of our nature come
In further evil?

Gone is the absolute fixation on the incestuous marriage; this is now only one of a set of grievances. Claudius must die, not out of mere revenge, but to prevent further harm from his evil nature. Further—Hamlet now sees the wisdom of patching up his quarrel with Laertes:

> But I am very sorry, good Horatio,
> That to Laertes I forgot myself;
> For, by the image of my cause, I see
> The portraiture of his. I'll court his favours.
> But sure, the bravery of his grief did put me
> Into a tow'ring passion.

With the return of insight, Hamlet can now put himself in Laertes' place and sense what he is feeling. His apology (for the death of Polonius and not the graveside incident) is a frank admission of past mental irresponsibility:

> Give me your pardon, sir, I have done you wrong;
> But pardon't, as you are a gentleman.
> This presence knows,
> And you must needs have heard, how I am punished
> With a sore distraction. What I have done,
> That might your nature, honour and exception
> Roughly awake, I here proclaim was madness.
> Was't Hamlet wronged Laertes? Never Hamlet.
> If Hamlet from himself be ta'en away,
> And when he's not himself does wrong Laertes,
> Then Hamlet does it not, Hamlet denies it.
> Who does it then? His madness. If't be so,
> Hamlet is of the faction that is wronged;
> His madness is poor Hamlet's enemy.
> Sir, in this audience,
> Let my disclaiming from a purposed evil
> Free me so far in your most generous thoughts,
> That I have shot my arrow o'er the house,
> And hurt my brother.

At this moment the play can still end happily. Moved by Hamlet's eloquent apology, Laertes has only to confess the poisoned foil and the instigation of the plot by Claudius. The pair of them, with Horatio, could form a triumvirate strong enough to bring down the King. Robert Speaight regards

Claudius as a more truly tragic figure than Hamlet; but what of Laertes? It is his weakness of character, matching that of his sister, that now ensures the catastrophe.

What seems a superfluity of corpses at the end is justified psychologically by Dr Ernest Jones's view that "because of his own repressed desire to possess his mother Hamlet cannot kill Claudius without killing himself, and therefore he can only do it when mortally wounded and the Queen is already dead and lost to him for ever." But the final scene is rarely dramatically effective. As an exception I can cite the Stratford production of 1948, when the audience was compelled to react introjectively to the lamentations of a terrified page; this is the only time that I have really felt the horror of the scene.

The summing up of Horatio is routine, but at least we have from Fortinbras this independent testimony to Hamlet's nobility:

> For he was likely, had he been put on,
> To have proved most royal.

We can agree with this and sense with horrified admiration the quick march of events at the moment when it had seemed that all might yet be well, with a Hamlet sane and capable of both judicious and judicial action. This emergence of a Hamlet, captain of his soul at last, but unable to be master of his fate, is the crowning glory of Shakespeare's genius in this play, and possibly in any other.

According to Sir Israel Gollancz, Shakespeare's main sources for the material of *Hamlet* are: the *Historica Danica* of Saxo Grammaticus, published in 1514; the *Histoires Tragicques* of Belleforest, 1582; and the near contemporary *Ur-Hamlet*, possibly by Kyd. Ernest Jones says that Shakespeare changed the earlier versions mainly by the introduction of the introspection and delaying, thus converting a simple drama into a profound internal conflict. Kenneth Muir notes that Belleforest mentions Amleth's "over-great melancholy", but the delay in this version is for the purpose of gaining time and allaying suspicion.

It is a matter of general agreement among the critics that the delay is the central feature of the drama. Lawrence Babb considers that Hamlet's melancholy would have been accepted by an Elizabethan audience as sufficient cause for this; Bradley is in agreement, but denies that the melancholy is an insane one.

I have quoted earlier from Timothy Bright. He describes the melancholy man as "pondering long and debating long"; but Ernest Jones does not accept the correspondence of Hamlet's symptoms with those given by Bright.

Robert Burton ranges so widely that one can find most forms of mental disorder comprehended by his generic classification of melancholy. He lists practically every unpleasant emotion and experience as a cause of melancholy, including desire of revenge. According to Burton, seeing spectres is "a corrupt phantasy". He mentions Orestes and the Furies, which he regards as a hallucination due to melancholy. He continues: "An object not well descried in the dark, fear and phantasy will suspect to be a ghost. . . . What the wretched overmuch desire they easily believe." Compare Theseus, in *A Midsummer Night's Dream*:

> For if they would but apprehend some joy,
> They comprehend the bringer of that joy;
> Or, in the night, imagining some fear,
> How easy is a bush supposed a bear.

Is this evidence that Burton was familiar with the plays of Shakespeare?

The conclusion is that Hamlet is a melancholy man by Elizabethan standards, but today we can be more precise. I can only understand the character and the play by inferring that he suffers from a true manic-depressive psychosis, with the following recognizable phases:

1. From the opening to the revelation of the Ghost, he is in a state of simple depression.
2. Agitated depression supervenes and lasts up to the end of the "nunnery" scene.
3. Mild elation, or hypomania, is the dominant mood throughout the scenes comprising the "Mousetrap" and the murder of Polonius.
4. On his return in Act V Hamlet is mentally normal and remains so until the end.

The apparent inconsistencies of the character are eliminated by understanding this sequence, which is sound psychopathology. The central problem, the delay, is only difficult if attempts are made to explain it on moral or complicated psychological grounds. Bradley is satisfied that the melancholy is an adequate cause, and psychiatry will support him.

If we agree that Hamlet suffers from a manic-depressive psychosis, it is not necessary to seek a cause for this. The condition, as we understand it, is constitutional and inborn; the environment is only a precipitating factor. It is said that pyknic, or round-headed, types are more prone to be manic-depressive: years of watching long-headed aesthetic actors in this part make us unmindful of indications in the text. Too much need not be made of "this too too solid flesh", which is commonly amended to "sullied"; but, in the final scene, Gertrude rather unkindly refers to Hamlet as "fat and scant of breath", giving support to the visualization by Shakespeare of a pyknic type. Possibly Burbadge was a little out of condition at the time.

The shock to Hamlet of his mother's marriage seems to me to have been over-emphasized. Granted that Elizabethans would have recognized it as incestuous, nobody in the play seems shocked but Hamlet, and I attribute his violent condemnation of Gertrude to his own highly charged emotional state.

It would be wearisome even to summarize the views of the Freudians on *Hamlet*. These are ingenious and interesting, but psycho-analysis of depressed patients is not usually considered helpful. Nevertheless, Freud's theory of the mechanism of melancholia may be considered apposite. According to this, the loss of a loved object by death or other cause may lead to a shifting of the libido and the sense of loss on to the ego, and so to nihilistic ideas. There is also an ambivalence by which the patient unconsciously wished for the death of the loved one and so reproaches himself for this. In the finality the ego may punish itself so severely that it causes its own death by suicide. When mania supervenes, the ego has surmounted the loss of the object, and is seeking wildly a new attachment for the free libido.

L. A. G. Strong regrets that Freud should have taken his terms from the Greek drama of predestination rather than from Shakespeare's drama of free choice: certainly the invocation of a "Hamlet" rather than an "Oedipus" complex would solve many problems for the critic.

Ernest Jones does not believe that Hamlet is a manic-depressive: his diagnosis is "cyclo-thymic hysteria". His views call for respect, particularly since he has shown himself to be an earnest Shakespearian scholar as well as a psychiatrist with a world-wide reputation. He does at least know what a neurosis is, an advantage denied to some of the literary critics.

In his delightful and generally profound study—*Nature in Shakespearean Tragedy*—I cannot understand why Robert Speaight refers to Hamlet as "the first neurotic". If neurosis is a modern conception, invented by the psychiatrists, Hamlet must be several centuries before his time; whereas if it is accepted that the word "neurotic" is a new coinage descriptive of an age-old reaction of mankind, then surely Adam and Eve must have precedence. As the result of eating the forbidden fruit they suffered from a typical neurosis of guilt; by a hysterical transference of this emotion to their bodies they became ashamed of their sexual organs—a sense of shame which has persisted in mankind to this day.

Harry Levin makes the vague diagnosis of "nervous breakdown", which is in fact an euphemism often used to cloak a severe and certifiable psychosis. He compares the madness of Hamlet with the maladjustment of Don Quixote, the misanthropy of Alceste and the idiocy of Prince Myshkin.

Bertram Joseph disagrees with the view of Ernest Jones that Hamlet "suffers an inhibition of the power to will in the particular direction of avenging his father's death". He introduces a moral and metaphysical slant by ascribing the delay to a knowledge that to obey an evil spirit and therefore slay a man is forbidden and will bring punishment after death.

After consideration of all these opinions and many others, I stand by my diagnosis of Hamlet's manic-depressive psychosis, with its succeeding phases, for all of which I have quoted authority from the text.

Although I do not agree that a search for deep motivation is necessary, there is in *Hamlet* a wealth of psychological symbolism in the treatment of the main character. I agree with Gilbert Murray that "far-flung myths, originating from deeper and darker origins among seasonal rites" converge in the tale; and that Hamlet has far more of Orestes than Oedipus in him. Gilbert Murray goes further—to suggest that the collective imagination rather than the individual ego is responsible for the power of the myth; which brings Hamlet more into line with the psychology of Jung than of Freud.

As early as 1925, Stopford Brooke, without using the specific

term, described Hamlet as an introverted type. He said that
Horatio, being of the same type, could understand him, whereas
the Queen, Polonius and Claudius—all extraverts—thought
him mad. Stopford Brooke, presumably an introvert himself,
finds no trace of madness in Hamlet, and considers that this idea
as an illusion of extraverted critics who do not understand a
character of the opposite type. In spite of this opinion, Stopford
Brooke admits that Hamlet is depressed, attributing this to a
normal reaction from his mother's remarriage.

I agree that the basic psychological orientation of the critics
is responsible for much of the divergence of their views. With
regard to Hamlet, he is clearly introverted, and the clue to his
dominant sub-type is in his cry: "O my prophetic soul! My
uncle!" His "prophetic soul" is the intuition which governs the
character. I have quoted some of the attributes of the introverted
intuitive in my chapter on Orsino. The complexity of Jung's
description when translated into English necessitates extended
quotation:

"The remarkable indifference of the extraverted intuitive in
respect to outer objects is shared by the introverted intuitive
in relation to the inner objects. Just as the extraverted intuitive
is continually scenting out new possibilities, which he pursues
with an equal unconcern both for his own welfare and for that of
others, pressing on quite heedless of human considerations,
tearing down what has only just been established in his ever-
lasting search for change, so the introverted intuitive moves
from image to image, chasing after every possibility in the
teeming womb of the unconscious, without establishing any
connection between the phenomenon and himself. Just as the
world can never become a moral problem for the man who
merely senses it, so the world of images is never a moral problem to the intuitive. To the one just as much as to the other it is
an aesthetic problem, a question of perception, a 'sensation'.
In this way the consciousness of his own bodily existence fades
from the introverted intuitive's view, as does his effect upon
others. The extraverted standpoint would say of him: 'Reality
has no existence for him; he gives himself up to fruitless phantasies.' A perception of the unconscious images, produced in
such inexhaustible abundance by the creative energy of life, is
of course fruitless from the standpoint of immediate utility. But,
since these images represent possible ways of viewing life, which

in given circumstances have the power to provide a new energic potential, this function, which to the outer world is the strangest of all, is as indispensable to the total psychic economy as is the corresponding human type to the psychic life of a people. Had this type not existed, there would have been no prophets in Israel.

"Introverted intuition apprehends the images which arise from the *a priori*, i.e. the inherited foundations of the unconscious mind. These archetypes, whose innermost nature is inaccessible to experience, represent the precipitate of psychic functioning of the whole ancestral line, i.e. the heaped-up, or pooled, experiences of organic existence in general, a million times repeated, and condensed into types.

"The peculiar nature of introverted intuition, when given the priority, also produces a peculiar type of man, viz.: the mystical dreamer and seer on the one hand, or the fantastical crank and artist on the other. . . . Intensification of intuition naturally often results in an extraordinary aloofness of the individual from tangible reality; he may even become an enigma to his own immediate circle. If an artist, he reveals extraordinary remote things in his art, which in iridescent profusion embrace both the significant and the banal, the lovely and the grotesque, the whimsical and the sublime. If not an artist, he is frequently an unappreciated genius, a great man 'gone wrong', a sort of wise simpleton, a figure for 'psychological' novels. Although it is not altogether in the line of the introverted intuitive type to make of perception a moral problem, since a certain reinforcement of the rational functions is required for this, yet even a relatively slight differentiation of judgement would suffice to transfer intuitive perception from the purely aesthetic into the moral sphere. A variety of this type is thus produced which differs essentially from its aesthetic form, although none the less characteristic of the introverted intuitive. The moral problem comes into being when the intuitive tries to relate himself to his vision, when he is no longer satisfied with mere perception and its aesthetic shaping and estimation, but confronts the question: what does this mean for me and for the world? What emerges from this vision in the way of a duty or task, either for me or for the world? The morally orientated intuitive concerns himself with the meaning of his vision; he troubles less about its further aesthetic possibilities than about the possible moral effects

which emerge from its intrinsic significance. His judgement
allows him to discern, though often only darkly, that he, as a
man, and as a totality, is in some way inter-related with his
vision, that it is something which cannot just be perceived but
which also would fain become the life of the subject. Through
this realization he feels bound to transform his vision into his
own life. But, since he tends to rely exclusively upon his vision,
his moral effort becomes one-sided; he makes himself and his
life symbolic, adapted it is true to the inner and eternal meaning
of events, but unadapted to the actual present-day reality.
Therewith he also deprives himself of any influence upon it,
because he remains unintelligible. His language is not that
which is commonly spoken—it becomes too subjective. His
argument lacks convincing reason. He can only confess or pro-
nounce. His is the 'voice of one crying in the wilderness'."

I find little difficulty in identifying Hamlet with the morally
orientated introverted intuitive. Only in his elated phase does
the impulsiveness and unrestraint of the repressed "sensation
of the object" take over, as it does in the neurotic phase of
Orsino, which I have described in the appropriate chapter.

One of Hamlet's problems seems to me to be a failure to
evolve a satisfactory "persona". He presents no protective front
to the world and so is the more capable of being wounded. He
suffers more from a fixation on his father than on his mother.
Here is his own word-picture:

> See what a grace was seated on this brow;
> Hyperion's curls, the front of Jove himself,
> An eye like Mars, to threaten and command;
> A station like the herald Mercury
> New lighted on a heaven-kissing hill:
> A combination and a form indeed,
> Where every god did seem to set his seal
> To give the world assurance of a man.

What greater contrast could there be between this dominating
extravert and his moody scholarly son? This incompatibility of
temperament, especially where there is a strong instinct for filial
devotion, breeds constant argument with the father in his lifetime and excessive remorse after his death. I find here a more
relevant background to Hamlet's melancholy than by the inference of an "Oedipus complex". The father's influence is
paramount in the development of a satisfactory front to the

world; Hamlet could not by his nature emulate his sire, but through the wish to do so failed in the evolution of a satisfactory "persona" for himself.

*Hamlet* is one of those plays in which the central character so occupies the attention that it is attractive to investigate the symbolic relationship of the other characters to him. In simple language: the Ghost represents Hamlet's conscience; the Freudians call it the super-ego, which is much the same thing. John Vyvyan sees a reflection of Hamlet in the phases of Ophelia: when he is noble she is pure; when his nobility totters she goes mad; when it is ruined she is drowned. According to Vyvyan, Polonius represents faith and loyalty—a role for which Horatio seems to me more apt. Finally, he cites Laertes as Hamlet's own vengeful force recoiling on himself.

It is possible to visualize the main characters according to the conception of Jung, as components of Hamlet's total psyche. Polonius and Gertrude thus appear as distorted forms of the archetypal wise old man and great mother; Ophelia is the anima, Claudius the dark shadow and the Ghost the persona. Only Horatio, as the helpful shadow, promotes any satisfactory stability in the psyche, and this structure expresses quite well the flaws responsible for the imperfect integration which we observe in Hamlet, and which is largely responsible for his failure to cope with the situation confronting him.

Dover Wilson associates the main characters with the political events of the year 1601, in which *Hamlet* is presumed to have been written. According to him, Hamlet represents Essex and Claudius Leicester, who was believed to have murdered the previous Earl of Essex before marrying his widow. Dover Wilson sees Burleigh in Polonius, and also notes that Shakespear's own father died in 1601.

But this kind of speculation, tribute though it be to Shakespeare's construction of a character at once so complex and so fascinating, is an exercise in psychological rumination that is sometimes perhaps taken too seriously. Harry Levin makes a sound point in surmising that Hamlet has a smack of each one of us in him, from which we derive an urge to put an interpretation on the character conforming to our own individual view rather than to Shakespeare's.

I will conclude my chapter by quoting Shakespeare's own views on the origin of psychological complexes, put into the mouth of Hamlet, and in which he actually uses the word "complexion", which remained dormant in this sense until resurrected by Freud three hundred years later:

> So, oft it chances in particular men
> That, for some vicious mole of nature in them,
> As, in their birth,—wherein they are not guilty,
> Since nature cannot choose his origin,—
> By their o'ergrowth of some complexion,
> Oft breaking down the pales and forts of reason,
> Or by some habit that too much o'er-leavens
> The form of plausive manners, that these men,—
> Carrying, I say, the stamp of one defect,
> Being nature's livery, or fortune's star,—
> Their virtues else—be they as pure as grace,
> As infinite as man may undergo—
> Shall in the general censure take corruption
> From that particular fault.

# 8

# TIMON—THE GENERAL PARALYTIC

VARIOUS dates between 1604 and 1608 have been allocated by the critics to this play. A connection has been suggested between the death of Shakespeare's brother, Edmund, in 1607 and the morbid content of the imagery. I am not concerned with dates, but I do regard *Timon* as a predecessor of *Lear*, and therefore written at the beginning rather than the end of the accepted period. T. W. Baldwin thinks that both plays were performed for the first time in 1605, and I am prepared to follow him.

The character of Timon is presented in an introductory dialogue between a Painter and a Poet, who function here as a chorus. Of melancholy characters in general I have already quoted Robert Burton as saying: "There is nothing so vain, absurd . . . so prodigious and strange, such as Painters and Poets durst not attempt, which they will not readily fear, feign, suspect and imagine unto themselves". The use by Shakespeare of these two characters representing the most imaginative of the arts to introduce his play foretokens the bizarre nature of the character and of the events which we are to witness.

A Jeweller has a precious stone for the great Lord Timon, and the Painter a magnificent portrait, but it is the Poet's book of praise which poses the character and reputation of Timon as the play opens. The first lines I have already quoted, in an earlier chapter:

> I have, in this rough work, shaped out a man,
> Whom this beneath world doth embrace and hug
> With amplest entertainment. My free drift
> Halts not particularly, but moves itself
> In a wide sea of wax. No levelled malice
> Infects one comma in the course I hold,
> But flies an eagle flight, bold and forth on,
> Leaving no tract behind.

The exposition continues:

> You see how all conditions, how all minds,
> As well of glib and slipping creatures as
> Of grave and austere quality, tender down
> Their services to Lord Timon. His large fortune,
> Upon his good and gracious nature hanging,
> Subdues and properties to his love and tendance
> All sorts of hearts; yea, from the glass-faced flatterer
> To Apemantus, that few things loves better
> Than to abhor himself . . .
> Sir, I have upon a high and pleasant hill
> Feigned Fortune to be throned: the base o' th' mount
> Is ranked with all deserts, all kind of natures,
> That labour on the bosom of this sphere
> To propagate their states: amongst them all,
> Whose eyes are on this sovereign lady fixed,
> One do I personate of Lord Timon's frame,
> Whom fortune with her ivory hand wafts to her;
> Whose present grace to present slaves and servants
> Translates his rivals . . .
> All those which were his fellows but of late,
> Some better than his value, on the moment
> Follow his strides, his lobbies fill with tendance,
> Rain sacrificial whisperings in his ear,
> Make sacred even his stirrup, and through him
> Drink the free air.

But flattery will not last:

> When Fortune in her shift and change of mood
> Spurns down her late beloved, all his dependants
> Which laboured after him to the mountain's top
> Even on their knees and hands, let him slip down,
> Not one accompanying his declining foot.

On Timon's entry, his first action is to pay a debt of five talents owed by Ventidius, and so release him from prison. Next he provides a dowry for his servant Lucilius so that he can wed a girl above his station. There follows a duologue with Apemantus, who berates him for his folly in yielding to flattery. But Timon continues on his profligate way. He refuses repayment from Ventidius, now made wealthy by his father's death; this causes surprise in us that a wealthy father should, in any case, have allowed a son to go to prison for a debt which he himself could easily have discharged.

At a magnificent banquet Timon states his creed of sharing among friends:

> We are born to do benefits: and what better or properer can
> we call our own than the riches of our friends? O, what a
> precious comfort 'tis to have so many like brothers com-
> manding one another's fortune! O, joy's e'en made away ere
> it can be born! Mine eyes cannot hold out water methinks:
> to forget their faults, I drink to you.

The thought of this universal brotherhood moves him to tears, emphasizing the emotional and impractical quality of his conception.

Whence did this wealth spring, that provided this splendid feast of wining and dancing? What is the source of this lavish generosity to all? Timon appears confident of a bottomless purse; not so his steward, Flavius:

> There's no crossing him in's humour;
> Else should I tell him—well, i'faith I should—
> When all's spent, he'ld be crossed then, and he could,
> 'Tis pity bounty had not eyes behind,
> That man might ne'er be wretched for his mind.

Flavius, like Horatio, is an utterly faithful character. He is in no plot to rob or discredit his master, and what he says may be believed implicitly. Later he elaborates on the situation:

> What will this come to?
> He commands us to provide and give great gifts,
> And all out of an empty coffer;
> Nor will he know his purse, or yield me this,
> To show him what a beggar his heart is,
> Being of no power to make his wishes good.
> His promises fly so beyond his state
> That what he speaks is all in debt, he owes
> For every word.

We need not accept the criticism of the cynical Apemantus, but Flavius exposes the whole position. Timon's wealth is non-existent—he is spending what he does not possess. Either he is operating a desperate confidence trick or the state of his mind must be suspect. It is clear, from any reading of the play, that the character is essentially noble, so that the first alternative may be dismissed. Timon is therefore in a state of pathological elation, patent to any physician. Whether this is part of a manic-depressive swing or due to some separate disease is not yet apparent, but delusions of boundless wealth are prominent in one specific brain infection; as there were no blood tests in Shakespeare's day, we must continue to seek evidence from the text.

Evidence, at least of a circumstantial nature, is forthcoming in Act II, Scene 2, which introduces a Fool and a Page, bearing letters from their mistress to Alcibiades and Timon. The Fool addresses the following remark to the usurers' men who are besieging Timon:

> I think no usurer but has a fool to his servant. My mistress is one, and I am her fool. When men come to borrow of your masters, they approach sadly and go away merry; but they enter my mistress' house merrily and go away sadly. . . .

It is clear that their mistress is a prostitute, and later passages show that Alcibiades has resort to these women. Why then should she send letters to Timon unless he were another of her clients? The reason for the sad departure of men from her house is not explained. Shakespeare may be implying nothing more than a transitory post-coital depression; but I consider it more likely that the sadness is a presage of infection with venereal disease. This otherwise insignificant passage provides definite textual evidence that Timon had run the risk of such infection.

In Act II the creditors are gathering. Timon owes thousands of talents, but seems oblivious of his position. He cannot understand why they should be so pressing, and courteously puts them off until another time. At last, alone with Flavius, he is made to realize the true state of his finances. Unwilling to admit his fault he projects the blame on to his servant:

> You make me marvel. Wherefore, ere this time,
> Had you not fully laid my state before me,
> That I might so have rated my expense
> As I had leave of means?

Flavius reminds him that he would not listen, drawing the grossly unfair rejoinder:

> Perchance some single vantages you took,
> When my indisposition put you back;
> And that unaptness made your minister
> Thus to excuse yourself.

Flavius defends himself with warmth and dignity; he is prepared to produce his books for any audit.

Brought to the understanding that even by the realization of his lands and all his possessions he could pay no more than half his debts, Timon determines to fall back upon his brotherhood of friends. Whilst his servants are scouring the city in a vain search for grateful protégés, we are introduced to three mysterious strangers, who comment in the fashion of a chorus. The First Stranger expresses an unequivocal opinion about the character of Timon:

> For mine own part,
> I never tasted Timon in my life,
> Nor came any of his bounties over me,
> To mark me for his friend; yet, I protest,
> For his right noble mind, illustrious virtue,
> And honourable carriage,
> Had his necessity made use of me,
> I would have put my wealth into donation,
> And the best half should have returned to him,
> So much I love his heart. But, I perceive,
> Men must learn now with pity to dispense,
> For policy sits above conscience.

Thus is Timon's nobility proclaimed by a disinterested, and therefore reliable, witness.

But for his credulous confidence in a generosity in others to match his own, Timon is at this point calm and reasonable. It is only when he realizes that he has not a single friend who will respond to his appeal that an abrupt and violent change of temper supervenes. He dismisses the creditors in a fit of rage, and plans a different kind of banquet for his erstwhile friends.

Meanwhile, in what appears to be a quite unrelated scene, Alcibiades, the soldier, is appealing to the Senate. A friend of Timon's, he is yet uninvolved in his financial difficulties; there is no record that he has been a recipient of Timon's bounty, nor of his appeal for help. Indeed, like a bluff soldier, at the earlier banquet he has spoken but three short sentences. The dramatic purpose of the scene in the Senate is no doubt to create suspense prior to the second banquet, and the practical purpose, as also in many of Shakespeare's fourth Acts, to give a rest to the leading actor. Symbolically, the banishment of Alcibiades by an ungrateful Senate for pleading for the life of a friend is a parallel to Timon's own misfortune, exhibiting a contrast between the reaction of the two characters to their experience of man's ingratitude.

H. J. Oliver draws the comparison between the successful, worldly Alcibiades and the noble, impractical Timon; this may also be regarded as the contrast between extraverted and introverted attitudes.

The speech of Alcibiades at his quittance of the Senators, though fully vituperant, is pitched in a lower key than the later fulminations of Timon:

> Now the gods keep you old enough, that you may live
> Only in bone, that none may look on you!
> I'm worse than mad. I have kept back their foes
> While they have told their money and let out
> Their coin upon large interest; I myself
> Rich only in large hurts. All those for this?
> Is this the balsam that the usuring Senate
> Pours into captain's wounds? Banishment!
> It comes not ill: I hate not to be banished.
> It is a cause worthy my spleen and fury,
> That I may strike at Athens. I'll cheer up
> My discontented troops, and lay for hearts.
> 'Tis honour with most lands to be at odds:
> Soldiers should brook as little wrongs as gods.

It is to be noted that the language is that of the soldier, haughty—but practical and resolute, with none of Timon's imagery of disease or depth of loathing.

It is now time to say a word about Apemantus, who is conjoined with Timon and Alcibiades to form a trio in opposition to the rest of Athens. His hatred of mankind is intellectual: he has no disillusionment, because he never had any expectations. Wyndham Lewis says that he has the function of a chorus expressing the criticism of the audience, but I think that his relation is specifically to Timon.

Apemantus tells us where he stands, by means of his grace with which he churlishly repulses Timon's hospitality at the first banquet:

> Immortal gods, I crave no pelf;
> I pray for no man but myself.
> Grant I may never prove so fond,
> To trust a man on his oath or bond,
> Or a harlot for her weeping.
> Or a dog that seems a sleeping,
> Or a keeper with my freedom,
> Or my friends, if I should need 'em.

> Amen, so fall to't.
> Rich men sin, and I eat root.

At the second banquet, Timon welcomes his friends with courtesy veiling sarcasm. When the dishes are uncovered the lid is truly off as he pelts them with stones and water:

> Live loathed, and long,
> Most smiling and smooth, detested parasites,
> Courteous destroyers, affable wolves, meek bears,
> You fools of fortune, trencher-friends, time's flies,
> Cap-and-knee slaves, vapours and minute-jacks!
> Of man and beast the infinite malady
> Crust you quite o'er! . . .

Here is the first mention of disease, which is to occupy so much of Timon's thought from now on. The "infinite malady" has been taken by some commentators to mean every kind of disease, but Sir St. Clair Thomson considers that it refers to syphilis, the "ultimate" in diseases, in the secondary stage of which appear various skin rashes sometimes leading to desquamation.

Timon's farewell to Athens is in the same strain:

> Let me look back on thee. O thou wall,
> That girdles in those wolves, dive in the earth,
> And fence not Athens! Matrons turn incontinent!
> Obedience fail in children! Slaves and fools,
> Pluck the grave wrinkled Senate from the bench,
> And minister in their steads! To general filths
> Convert o' th' instant, green virginity!
> Do't in your parents' eyes! Bankrupts, hold fast:
> Rather than render back, out with your knives,
> And cut your trusters' throats! Bound servants steal!
> Large-handed robbers your grave masters are
> And pill by law. Maid, to thy master's bed!
> Thy mistress is o' th' brothel. Son of sixteen,
> Pluck the lined crutch from thy old limping sire,
> With it beat out his brains! Piety and fear,
> Religion to the gods, peace, justice, truth,
> Domestic awe, night-rest and neighbourhood,
> Instruction, manners, mysteries and trades,
> Degrees, observances, customs and laws,
> Decline to your confounding contraries,
> And yet confusion live! Plagues incident to men,
> Your potent and infectious fevers heap
> On Athens, ripe for stroke! Thou cold sciatica,

Cripple our senators, that their limbs may halt
As lamely as their manners! Lust and liberty
Creep in the minds and manners of our youth,
That 'gainst the stream of virtue they may strive,
And drown themselves in riot! Itches, blains,
Sow all th' Athenian bosoms, and their crop
Be general leprosy! Breath infect breath,
That their society, as their friendship, may
Be merely poison! Nothing I'll bear from thee
But nakedness, thou detestable town!
Take thou that too, with multiplying bans!
Timon will to the woods, where he shall find
The unkindest beast more kinder than mankind.
The gods confound—hear me, you good gods all!—
Th' Athenians both within and out that wall!
And grant, as Timon grows, his hate may grow
To the whole race of mankind, high and low!
Amen.

I have quoted the whole of this long speech, including the significant "amen" at the end, for several reasons. One is to show the contrast between the brief, practical eloquence of Alcibiades and Timon's inconclusive nihilism. Alcibiades has said all that is necessary, but Timon is to continue in the same strain for the rest of the play.

Another reason is my wish to discuss the references to prostitution and disease without being accused of theorizing apart from the context.

The similarities of and differences between early Jacobean life and our own are well recorded in this speech. Rebellion in children was evidently a matter for scandal in Shakespeare's day, and not the commonplace of our society; but we still find shocking the idea of the sexual corruption of youth.

It is not easy to transcribe to modern terminology all the symptoms of disease which Timon invokes. "Pill", of course, is "pillage"—nothing to do with medicine—and the word "stroke" is not used in a medical sense. Sciatica, as we understand it, is in no way "cold", and it is more likely that Timon is referring to circulatory disease of the legs, which, although caused also by other conditions, is a recognized complication of syphilis. Similarly, the "blains" and "general leprosy" are more likely to refer to syphilitic ulcers than to the affections understood by these words today.

Timon's hatred of mankind—*vide* the final "amen"—has
now become a religion, spreading beyond the confines of
Athens, all-embracing and altogether disproportionate even to
his earlier exuberance and lavish designs for a new brotherhood
of man.

Already we might feel that the character has stepped too far
beyond the margin of credibility to sustain our interest; but, as
if to rebuke and to remind us of the inherent nobility of the
mentally deformed creature which we are to follow to the woods,
there come his servants, moved to pity by the fate of their
master, when we might expect their main concern to be for their
own loss of employment. These are the phrases which come
from them:

> So noble a master fall'n! All gone! and not
> One friend to take his fortune by the arm,
> And go along with him!
>
> . . . . . . . . . . . . . . . . . . . . . . .
>                         And his poor self,
> A dedicated beggar to the air,
> With his disease of all-shunned poverty,
> Walks, like contempt, alone . . .

Following the precepts of his master, Flavius divides his own
small fortune with the others:

>                         Good fellows all,
> The latest of my wealth I'll share amongst you.
> Wherever we shall meet, for Timon's sake
> Let's yet be fellows: let's shake our heads and say,
> As 'twere a knell unto our master's fortunes,
> 'We have seen better days.' Let each take some.

Timon's exhortation on the brotherhood of man has not fallen
entirely on stony ground.

There follows a soliloquy by Flavius on his master's fate:

> . . . Poor honest lord, brought low by his own heart,
> Undone by goodness! Strange, unusual blood,
> When man's worst sin is, he does too much good!
> Who then dares to be half so kind again?
> For bounty, that makes gods, does still mar men.
> My dearest lord, blest to be most accursed,
> Rich only to be wretched, thy great fortunes
> Are made thy chief afflictions. Alas, kind lord!
> He's flung in rage from this ungrateful seat

Of monstrous friends; nor has he with him to
Supply his life, or that which can command it.
I'll follow, and inquire him out.
I'll ever serve his mind with my best will;
Whilst I have gold, I'll be his steward still.

Not a word about Timon's profligacy, nor his refusal to face the
facts of his indebtedness before it was too late; not a reproach
for Timon's mistrust of his stewardship.

Samuel Johnson says that "Nothing contributes more to the
exaltation of Timon's character than the fidelity of his servants.
Nothing but real virtue can be honoured by domestics. Nothing
but impartial kindness can gain affection from dependents."
Could this estimate be made of Timon from what has appeared
in the text of the play so far? There is something missing—the
earlier history of the man, before he impoverished himself with
such reckless generosity. Unless his fortune were originally that
of Croesus, he could hardly have survived long the improvidence
shown from the beginning of the play. There is therefore a
strong presumption that he had a prior and more normal
existence, in which his communistic ideas kept pace with his
means, and his generosity expressed itself in such simple acts of
kindness as would have endeared him to his servants. I cannot
believe that we are meant to regard him as in his normal mental
health at the opening of the play.

Timon is next observed in the woods near Athens, digging for
roots to eat, and finding, ironically, that most coveted by others
but now most despised by him: gold. His first visitors are Alcibiades with two courtesans, Phrynia and Timandra. There can
be no doubt of the status of these women. It might be presumed
that to Timon in his misanthropic temper all the female popula-
tion of the world are prostitutes; but, in fact, Timandra is specifically mentioned in Plutarch's *Life of Alcibiades* as a courtesan,
with whom he was living at the time of his death. According to
Plutarch, Alcibiades was morally ruined by the homosexual
practices current in Greece. A youth of outstanding physical
beauty, he exercised a power over older men equivalent to that
of the *femme fatale* in modern literature. One of the favourites
of Socrates, he also appears with Timon in Plutarch's *Life of
Antony*, in which Timon shuns all but the company of Alcibiades
—"a bold and insolent youth, whom he would greatly feast
and make much of, and kissed him very gladly."

Apart from the character of Timandra, Shakespeare makes no use of this material. There is no suggestion of any improper relationship between Timon and Alcibiades, and the imagery in the play is entirely heterosexual. But the theme of prostitution is important. If the contrasts in *Timon* are solely those between wealth and poverty, true friends and time-servers, aggression and submission, gold and roots, why does not Shakespeare keep on this unexceptional plane? The recurrent imagery of sores and disease and the withering verbal assault on the prostitutes seem unnecessary, unless there is some deeper injury which Timon has received from the world than the loss of his fortune and his reputed friends.

After a brief condemnation of war, Timon tells Alcibiades that:

> This fell whore of thine
> Hath in her more destruction than thy sword,
> For all her cherubin look.

This is a plain intimation that she is infected with venereal disease, accentuated by the accusation that a kiss from her will cause the lips to rot. He speaks to Timandra in similar vein:

> Be a whore still. They love thee not that use thee:
> Give them diseases, leaving with thee their lust.
> Make use of thy salt hours. Season the slaves
> For tubs and baths; bring down rose-cheek'd youth
> To the tub-fast and the diet.

Later there follows a masterly and dramatic description of some of the commoner effects of syphilis in the tertiary stage:

> Consumptions sow
> In hollow bones of man; strike their sharp shins,
> And mar men's spurring. Crack the lawyer's voice,
> That he may never more false title plead,
> Nor sound his quillets shrilly. Hoar the flamen
> That scolds against the quality of flesh
> And not believes himself. Down with the nose,
> Down with it flat; take the bridge quite away
> Of him that, his particular to foresee,
> Smells from the general weal. Make curled-pate ruffians bald;
> And let the unscarred braggarts of the war
> Derive some pain from you. Plague all,
> That your activity may defeat and quell
> The source of all erection. There's more gold:

Do you damn others, and let this damn you,
And ditches grave you all.

It is not necessary to reduce Timon's catalogue to precise
medical terms. Shakespeare's observation of the tertiary stage of
syphilis, though naturally incomplete, is meticulously accurate.

Alcibiades endures all this with exemplary patience, promising
to visit Timon again if his assault on Athens should prove
successful.

Apemantus is the next visitor. He describes Timon's attitude
as a "poor unmanly melancholy sprung from change of fortune",
and counsels him to mend his state by becoming a flatterer
himself. He judges that Timon's exile is enforced by poverty—
not voluntary—and therefore not commendable:

> If thou didst put this sour cold habit on
> To castigate thy pride, 'twere well: but thou
> Does it enforcedly. Thou'dst courtier be again,
> Wert thou not beggar. Willing misery
> Outlives incertain pomp, is crowned before.
> The one is filling still, never complete,
> The other at high wish. Best state, contentless,
> Hath a distracted and most wretched being,
> Worse than the worst, content.
> Thou shouldst desire to die, being miserable.

Timon points out that Apemantus was born miserable, and so
has had to endure no change of fortune himself:

> Thy nature did commence in sufferance, time
> Hath made thee hard in't. Why shouldst thou hate men?
> They never flattered thee. What hast thou given?
> If thou wilt curse, thy father, that poor rag,
> Must be thy subject, who in spite put stuff
> To some she beggar and compounded thee
> Poor rogue hereditary . . .

Breaking through the professional impassivity of Apemantus, he
succeeds in making him lose his temper. The abuse they hurl at
each other degenerates into simple monosyllables: Beast!"—
"Slave!"—"Toad!"—"Rogue!", for all the world like two
preparatory schoolboys.

Apemantus is not seen again. His cynicism has been exposed
and found wanting.

Three bandits now arrive, who are almost converted from

their thieving by Timon's encouragement of it, in line with our experience of the mentality which must be "agin the government". Timon bids them:

> Trust not the physician:
> His antidotes are poison, and he slays
> More than you rob.

Until the recent advent of penicillin this might have been particularly alleged of the remedies against syphilis, which required prolonged and painful treatment. "A day with Bacchus, a night with Venus, and three years with Mercury" used to be a favourite aphorism in medical circles.

An unwilling welcome is forced on Timon for his faithful servant, Flavius, but he has to rationalize his temporary abandonment of total misanthropy by maintaining that the tears of Flavius make him a woman, who has rejected man's estate as Timon has himself—a piece of sophistry which ignores the comprehensive nature of the term "mankind".

Alone to Flavius Timon gives gold for his true enrichment:

> Look thee, 'tis so! thou singly honest man,
> Here, take. The gods, out of my misery,
> Has sent thee treasure. Go, live rich and happy;
> But thus conditioned: thou shalt build from men,
> Hate all, curse all, show charity to none,
> But let the famished flesh slide from the bone
> Ere thou relieve the beggar. Give to dogs
> What thou deniest to men: let prisons swallow 'em,
> Debts wither 'em to nothing. Be men like blasted woods,
> And may diseases lick up their false bloods!
> And so farewell, and thrive.

In dismissing Flavius to the world outside, Timon appears to have enough insight to realize that, for the lone honest man, there is more peril in the woods than among the hated and despised Athenians.

In the last Act the Poet and Painter reappear, not this time as a chorus to interpret Timon to the audience, but as average representatives of his flattering friends. Learning of the distribution of his newly found largesse they plan to be taken back into his favour. Nothing could serve better to show Timon that the world is still what it was, and so confirm him in the misanthropy perhaps slightly shaken by the visit from Flavius.

After beating away the flatterers Timon receives a deputation from Athens, the more doomed to failure from what has immediately preceded it. The senators offer him absolute power if he will return to rally the Athenians against Alcibiades. In his refusal something has departed of Timon's vituperative flow:

> If Alcibiades kill my countrymen,
> Let Alcibiades know this of Timon,
> That Timon cares not. But if he sack fair Athens,
> And take our goodly aged men by th' beards,
> Giving our holy virgins to the stain
> Of contumelious, beastly, mad-brained war,
> Then let him know, and tell him Timon speaks it,
> In pity of our aged and our youth,
> I cannot choose but tell him, that I care not,
> And let him take't at worst . . .

The reason for this softening of his invective is a weary consciousness of the approach of death:

> Why, I was writing of my epitaph:
> It will be seen tomorrow. My long sickness
> Of health and living now begins to mend,
> And nothing brings me all things. Go, live still,
> Be Alcibiades your plague, you his,
> And last you long enough.

By this we understand that Timon rejoices in his failing health, welcoming the release of death. For the Athenians he has this one comfort to offer: a tree whereon they may conveniently hang themselves.

Dover Wilson compares the tragedy of Hamlet—in being struck down when he has recovered his mental poise—with that of Timon—impotent to recover when recovery is needed to save Athens.

Timon's final lines leave uncertain the mode of his dying, which might as well be from disease as from suicide:

> Come not to me again; but say to Athens,
> Timon hath made his everlasting mansion
> Upon the beached verge of the salt flood;
> Who once a day with his embossed froth
> The turbulent surge shall cover. Thither come,
> And let my gravestone be your oracle.
> Lips, let sour words go by and language end.
> What is amiss, plague and infection mend!

> Graves only be men's works, and death their gain!
> Sun, hide thy beams! Timon hath done his reign.

At the end of the play, the triumphant Alcibiades is brought an impression of Timon's epitaph, found by his grave on the sea-shore. Of how he died there is no indication, nor by what hand he was buried:

> Here lies a wretched corse, of wretched soul bereft.
> Seek not my name. A plague consume you wicked caitiffs left!
> Here lie I, Timon, who, alive, all living men did hate.
> Pass by and curse thy fill, but pass and stay not here thy gait.

These twin epitaphs, the second contradicting the anonymity of the first, are generally considered to be alternative versions conjoined; the origin of the second is from the poet Callimachus. I am not qualified to argue matters of text—in any case they add little to our evaluation of Timon or Timon's of himself.

Alcibiades adds his own envoi:

> These well express in thee thy latter spirits.
> Though thou abhorr'dst in us our human griefs,
> Scornedst our brain's flow and those droplets which
> From niggard nature fall, yet rich conceit
> Taught thee to make vast Neptune weep for aye
> On thy low grave, on faults forgiven. Dead
> Is noble Timon, of whose memory
> Hereafter more . . .

These words, together with the appeal of the senators, confirm the possession at one time by Timon of a nobility which could not be directly inferred from his behaviour in any part of the play. This could be no mere squanderer of collected or inherited wealth, who disowned the world when his fortunes failed him; but a man at one time of prudent counsel and admired virtue, a distinguished servant of his country.

Shakespeare's sources for the play *Timon* are a matter for dispute. Paul Stapfer says that it shows evidence of copying from North's translation of Plutarch, itself taken from the French translation of Amyot. Wyndham Lewis describes his main inspiration as from Lucian's *Timon the Misanthrope*, invoking the lack of any known translation in Shakespeare's time as evidence of the absurdity of Ben Jonson's criticism of his "small Latin and Less Greek". But J. C. Maxwell avers that Lucian had already been translated into Latin, Italian and

French! In Lucian's work Timon is a prodigal, reduced to poverty by flatterers, who flock back to him when he digs up a treasure of gold.

Robert Burton, in his general description of melancholy, mentions *Timon the Misanthrope* by name as an example of the type of melancholic who delights in floods, waters and desert places, averse to company. He also describes a type who: "fears all old women as witches . . . every person comes near him is maleficiated, every creature, all intend to hurt him, seek his ruin." In Burton's classification Timon would provide an example of true saturnine melancholy, which causes "sadness and solitariness—fear—suspicion—dreams of graves, death and think themselves dead." Among the causes of melancholy, but without elaboration, he lists the "French pox", which was known in other parts as the "Neapolitan" and sometimes the "English" disease. There is no suggestion that Burton was familiar with Shakespeare's *Timon*, but he had certainly studied Lucian.

Lawrence Babb describes Timon as acidly melancholy: "His psychic disorder is due to a mistaken faith in human nature; his quarrel with the world is valid." He regards Timon as an honest malcontent and Apemantus as a satirical one.

Wyndham Lewis sees in Timon "a violent and mournful despair in a great nature full of generosity, in a time of awakening and immense astonishment at the vileness of the world".

Wilson Knight notes the mental division of the "problem" plays: "On the one side an exquisite apprehension of the spiritual—beauty, romance, poetry; on the other, the hate theme, loathing of the impure, aversion from the animal kinship of man, disgust at the decaying body of death. This dualism is resolved in the tragedies: the hate theme itself is finely sublimated in *Timon* by means of that purification of great passion, human grandeur and all the panoply of high tragedy."

Whilst not denying the validity of the moral and poetic values of the play, I believe that the evidence of Timon's principal problem is incontrovertible; and it is primarily a physical problem—the infection of his brain by syphilitic disease. The boundless largesse, the delusions of grandeur, the omnipotence expressed as much in his hatred as in his love—all these together might not be decisive; but, accompanied as they are by the recurrent imagery drawn from the classical symptomatology of syphilitic disease in all its stages, bring us to a conclusion which, however much we may dislike it, we cannot reasonably reject.

On searching the literature I have been astonished to find that this conclusion, reached by Dr Somerville in 1929, has been persistently glossed over by other critics. In his foreword to Dr Somerville's book—*Madness in Shakespearean Tragedy*—Wyndham Lewis rejects this diagnosis, relying on the atypical picture in the latter part of the play and ignoring the absolutely characteristic description at the beginning. It is natural that literary critics should prefer the behaviour of the characters which they dissect to be based on strictly moral and ethical considerations, rather than on some mental abnormality of which they have little knowledge. But Shakespeare is not so accommodating. He did not present his characters for their motives to be neatly analysed; he depicted men as he found them, and he had a wide acquaintance with the mentally abnormal. It cannot be maintained that dramatic art requires motivation to be based strictly on the principle of free choice. The tragedies that result from a diseased mind are as moving and dramatically as absorbing as those proceeding from an ethically defective judgement, provided that the character is inherently noble and worthy of our attention.

Aristotle says that tragedy should aim to depict people as better than they actually are. It is a "representation of an action that is heroic, complete and of a certain magnitude—by means of language enriched with all kinds of ornament". It is in these respects that I find it difficult to interest myself in much of the work of modern English playwrights. However perceptive the characterization, the "common man" and his everyday language cannot evoke that mingled sense of pity and admiration with which we follow the characters of Shakespeare's tragedies through all their adversities, including those such as Timon, whose choice is limited by defects of feeling or reason over which they have no voluntary control.

Arthur Sewell says that there is general agreement that in Shakespeare's tragedies we "witness a form of chemical change in the hero's spirit, brought about by a situation which makes demands on him which he cannot fulfil, and by a moral failure which has its issue at last in a reorganization of his own being." But he considers that Timon's misanthropy is morally disproportionate and psychologically unconvincing, thus admitting that in this tragedy there is an element inaccessible to analysis on moral grounds.

It is Shakespeare's art to persuade us of Timon's greatness and his worth as a tragic character by words of mouth alone. This word of mouth comprises the opinions and the attitudes of his friends and servants, enhanced by the language of his own utterances, whether in elation or despair, conveying a sense of the desperate struggle which is racking him from within his brain. But it is not a moral struggle nor one of decision—it is the struggle to preserve his sanity; and no less deeply moving for that. At no time in the play is there any hesitation or conflict over a decision he has to make. In fact he makes but one decision of importance to the drama. Once his bankruptcy is inevitable and the falseness of his friends exposed, he decides to have nothing further to do with the world of men. Not the discovery of a new source of wealth in the soil; not the appeals of his true friend Alcibiades and his faithful servant Flavius; not the intimation that Athens still honours and needs him—none of these can shake for one moment his inflexible resolve.

The Timon of the first three Acts is not credible as a noble and generous person. It is easy to be generous with other people's money, as taxpayers and ratepayers often know to their cost. It is clear that Timon has borrowed heavily and widely, and that his brotherhood of man is a pathetic sham—a hyperbole in keeping with his other extravagant ideas. In his search for aid he is equally unpractical: his request to the Senate for a thousand pounds on the instant is like trying to extract a million pounds from the Chancellor of the Exchequer without any parliamentary vote.

Dr Somerville is in some difficulty over the second half of the play, because it is more usual to find in dementia paralytica a benign and friendly attitude throughout. He points out, and I agree with him, that Timon's sense of omnipotence is the important factor in maintaining the diagnosis; whereas he was formerly omnipotent in his benevolence, his malevolence becomes equally boundless.

It is useful to compare Timon's state of mind with that of Hamlet, of whom Coleridge considered Timon to be an "after-vibration, written directly afterwards". The difference seems to me that, whereas in Hamlet the changes are those of fundamental temperament, Timon's only alteration is of the mood in

which his temperament is expressed. William McDougall
defines temperament as "the sum of the effects upon his (a
man's) mental life of the metabolic changes that are constantly
going on in all the tissues of his body". As a result of these
changes Hamlet is at different times sluggish, quick, excitable
and stable; Timon is excitable and impetuous throughout—it is
the mood that alters from benevolent to irascible. McDougall
refers to moods as "an affective-conative fact of immediate
experience", usually transitory. But in "cases of long persistent
morbid moods, we naturally suspect the presence of an organic factor", which seems to be applicable in the case of
Timon's fixed misanthropy.

I join L. A. G. Strong in regarding this misanthropy psychologically as a projection on to the world of Timon's dislike of
himself for what he has become. It is not the ingratitude of his
friends but the dim awareness of his own profligacy which
drives him from Athens. He knows that his mind can never be
restored to normality and that all he has to look forward to is
dementia followed by death. His abuse of the prostitutes,
though couched in general terms, is not for what they have done
to men in general, but to himself in particular.

Margaret Webster considers that Shakespeare must have
been mentally and spiritually rudderless when he wrote *Timon*;
Wilson Knight compares Shakespeare with Tolstoy, who at one
time admitted that life had become for him completely without
meaning. But I do not think it necessary to impute to Shakespeare any personal motive in his presentation of the character.
If he himself were in a deeply depressed mood he would hardly
be capable of such artistic creation, and he certainly would not
wish to draw attention to a disease of which he had become a
victim. Similarly I do not attach any importance to the recent
death of his brother Edmund. No one with Shakespeare's
natural delicacy of feeling would advertise to the world a
family tragedy of this nature. Shakespeare was deeply interested
in observing and recording everything which he found about
him, applying to previously ill-defined characters drawn re-
motely from history the effects of morbid psychological and
physical conditions impressed upon him from his own environment.

I agree with J. C. Maxwell that *Timon* may be a sketch for
the subsequent *Lear*, which would account for its loose con-

struction and lack of dramatic quality. Lear, also, may be regarded as suffering from an organic disease of the brain, a senile dementia, causing the same over-confidence in the honesty and integrity of mankind; the same shocked embitterment is apparent, culminating in a mental collapse more complete and more prolonged.

It is not necessary to seek for further unconscious motivation in *Timon*, but there is an abundance of psychologically important imagery. Wilson Knight finds three forces in the play: Timon, the transcendent lover, Mankind, the bride of his soul, and Apemantus, the devil of cynicism. He poses the same relationship between Lear, Cordelia and Edmund—Othello, Desdemona and Iago—Troilus, Cressida and Thersites—The Duke, Isabella and Lucio. Ultimately, he says, the hero in these plays represents mankind, the villain the devil and the loved one the divine principle.

In Freudian terms, Apemantus is Timon's super-ego and Alcibiades his ego-ideal. In the latter part of the play Timon himself appears to be a representation of the id, buried in the depths of the unconscious symbolized by the woods and the seashore.

Jung's psychology gives more scope for differentiating between separate aspects of the personality. I visualize the Timon of the earlier part as a detachment of the persona, the generous person shown to the world. The later Timon veers to the opposite extreme—the shadow buried in the unconscious; the tempter able to bribe with gold. Apemantus may be another distorted form of the wise old man. The good aspect of the anima is missing, but Phrynia and Timandra are there to represent the seductress. Alcibiades and Flavius may be regarded as helpful aspects of the shadow.

This kind of approach is, of course, entirely conjectural, but there is an increasing tendency, as Shakespeare's art matures, for subsidiary characters to group themselves round the central figure, often in an easily recognizable symbolical relationship.

In view of critical opinion on the lack of co-ordination and the imperfect structure of *Timon of Athens*, it is appropriate here to consider the play in relation to ancient and modern views on tragic form.

Aristotle divides a tragedy into four parts:

1. The Protasis, or entrance, which sheds light only on the character of the hero.
2. The Epistasis, or working up.
3. The Catastasis, or height and full growth of the play.
4. The Catastrophe, or dénouement.

In *Timon*, the Protasis occupies Act I, in which Timon is shown dispensing hospitality which he cannot afford. The Epistasis includes Act II and the first scenes of Act III, showing Timon's fruitless efforts to evade ruin. The Catastasis starts with the second banquet and continues up to the end of Act V, Scene 1, leaving as the Catastrophe the triumph of Alcibiades and the death of Timon. Shakespeare seems to conform fairly closely to the demands of Aristotle, with the exception that the Catastasis is too long drawn out.

According to John Vyvyan, Shakespeare's way of conceiving tragedy is more complicated:

"1. We are shown a soul, in many respects noble, with a fatal flaw.
2. The voices of the coming temptation are shown, and we know that they will persuade to evil.
3. The hero is tempted and yields.
4. An inner conflict, usually a soliloquy, in which the native nobility opposes the temptation, but fails.
5 and 6. A second temptation and a second conflict, as the result of which the hero loses the kingship of his own soul.
7. The tragic act of darkness.
8. Realization of horror.
9. Death."

In the case of *Timon*, stage 1 shows him with his fatal over-generosity. In stages 2 and 3, telescoped, we know that he is spending more than he possesses. Stage 4 is missing. There is substituted the desperate attempt by Timon to rectify his position; his failure is only his fault in so far as it is due to his unjustified confidence in his friends. The second temptation, in stages 5 and 6, may be represented by the despair and hatred to which Timon yields instead of rousing his courage to start afresh; but there is no conflict. The tragic act of darkness is the flight to the woods, which stages 8 and 9 follow automatically.

This attempt to relate *Timon* to John Vyvyan's sequence is not very successful. The dramatic imperfections of the play arise from the compression of the earlier part, in which we never see the reasonable, noble Timon, and the prolongation into two Acts of the final phase. This is not a necessity from the character of the hero, to which, however, Shakespeare still keeps faith by concluding with the inevitable physical and mental dissolution.

Timon's "psychological type" can only be tentatively inferred, because, as I have explained, we never see him in his normal health; but the character effecting the actions which we observe in the play conforms in many respects to the introverted sensation type.

Wilson Knight gives a lead, in describing Timon's world as "sensuous and erotic, yet not vicious or ignoble. His love is a rich erotic perception welling up from his soul . . . as is the love of Shakespeare for the fair boy of the Sonnets". It is "directed not towards one creature or one purpose, but expanding its emotion among all men" (i.e. introverted).

Jung's description of the introverted sensation type is as follows:

"It is an irrational type, inasmuch as its selection among occurrences is not primarily rational, but is guided rather by just what happens. Whereas the extraverted sensation type is determined by the intensity of the objective influence, the introverted type is orientated by the intensity of the subjective sensation-constituent released by the objective stimulus. Obviously, therefore, no sort of proportional relation exists between object and sensation, but something that is apparently quite irregular and arbitrary. . . . If there were present a capacity and readiness for expression in any way commensurate with the strength of sensation, the irrationality of this type would be extremely evident. . . . But, since this is the exception, it usually happens that the characteristic difficulty of introverted expression also conceals his irrationality. . . . Thus, this type becomes an affliction to his circle, just in so far as his entire harmlessness is no longer above suspicion. But, if the latter should be the case, the individual readily becomes a victim to the aggressiveness and ambitions of others. Such men allow themselves to be abused, for which they usually take vengeance at the most unsuitable moments with redoubled stubbornness and resistance. . . . This type, therefore, is commonly inaccessible to an objective understanding; and he fares no better in the understanding of himself. Above all, his development estranges him from the reality of the object, handing him over to his subjective perceptions, which orientate his consciousness in accordance with an archaic reality, although his deficiency in comparative judgement keeps him wholly unaware of this fact. Actually he moves in a mythological world, where men, animals, houses, rivers and mountains appear partly as benevolent deities and partly as malevolent demons. That thus they appear to him never enters his mind, although their effect upon his judgement and acts can bear no other interpretation. He judges and acts as though he had such powers to deal with; but this begins to strike him only when he discovers that his sensations are totally different from reality. . . .

"His unconscious is distinguished chiefly by the repression of intuition, which thereby acquires an extraverted and archaic character. Whereas true extraverted intuition has a characteristic resourcefulness, and a 'good nose' for every possibility in objective reality, this archaic, extraverted intuition has an amazing flair for every ambiguous, gloomy, dirty and dangerous possibility in the background of reality. . . . So long as the individual is not too aloof from the object, the unconscious intuition effects a wholesome compensation to the rather fantastic and over-credulous attitude of consciousness. But as soon as the unconscious becomes antagonistic to consciousness, such intutions come to the surface and expand their nefarious influence: they force themselves compellingly upon the individual, releasing compulsive ideas about objects of the most perverse kind. The neurosis arising from this sequence of events is usually a compulsion neurosis, in which the hysterical characters recede and are obscured by symptoms of exhaustion."

Setting aside difficulties in the translation and the technical verbiage, this description is in astonishingly apt relationship with the contrasting phases of Timon. The inference is that, although fundamentally irrational, his conscious attitude allows him to lead a reasonably normal existence until the realization that he has been exploited causes a mental breakdown, putting the unconscious extraverted intuition in control.

The adduction of this kind of psychopathological mechanism does not contradict the parallel operation of syphilitic disease on the brain.

# 9

## PERICLES—THE SCHIZOPHRENIC

*Pericles* is one of Shakespeare's least popular plays, but the main character is of some interest in my series, as it exemplifies a degree of melancholy productive of prolonged stupor.

I am not concerned with textual criticism, in which many of the commentators on this play have become so entangled that there has been little penetration of its psychological and symbolic content. I accept that the first two Acts are not primarily Shakespeare's, and I cannot believe that he was responsible for the affected archaism of the Chorus—Gower. Kenneth Muir suggests that Laurence Twine's *Pattern of Painful Adventures* is the root source, but that the general construction of the latter part is typically Shakespeare's own. Although the language of the play changes after Act II, the character of Pericles can be followed as a coherent entity throughout, and I regard the melancholy of the earlier part as a precursor of the stupor which occurs later.

At the start of the play Pericles is a classically heroic figure. He is prepared to risk the death which has overtaken all the previous suitors—for the love of a fair lady. To her father's warning he replies:

> Antiochus, I thank thee, who hath taught
> My frail mortality to know itself,
> And by those fearful objects to prepare
> This body, like to them, to what I must;
> For death remembered should be like a mirror,
> Who tells us life's but breath, to trust it error.
> I'll make my will then, and as sick men do,
> Who know the world, see heaven, but feeling woe
> Gripe not at earthly joys as erst they did,
> So I bequeath a happy peace to you
> And all good men, as every prince should do;

My riches to the earth from whence they came;
But my unspotted fire of love to you (to the princess)
Thus ready for the way of life or death,
I wait the sharpest blow, Antiochus.

I quote at length because, whoever wrote the actual lines, the character of the hero is clearly proclaimed, as is Shakespeare's wont, at the outset of the play.

Here is the riddle which Pericles must solve—or die:

I am no viper, yet I feed
On mother's flesh which did me breed.
I sought a husband, in which labour
I found that kindness in a father.
He's father, son, and husband mild;
I mother, wife, and yet his child.
How they may be, and yet in two,
As you will live, resolve it you.

Apart from the extension of the relationship to cover three generations there is no difficulty in the solution—one marvels at the obtuseness of the previous suitors! The reaction of Pericles is natural: turning pale in his revulsion he makes it clear to Antiochus that he has solved the riddle, but that a direct answer would be undiplomatic:

Kings are earth's gods: in vice their law's their will;
And if Jove stray, who dares say Jove doth ill?
It is enough you know; and it is fit,
What being more known grows worse, to smother it.
All love the womb that their first being bred,
Then give my tongue like leave to love my head.

Antiochus, pretending that he does not understand, gives Pericles a respite of forty days, so that he can decide on his own next move. Left alone, Pericles (who already knows the fate of the earlier suitors!) ponders on the moral outlook which his new knowledge of Antiochus has revealed:

One sin, I know, another doth provoke:
Murther's as near to lust as flame to smoke.
Poison and treason are the hands of sin,
Ay, and the targets, to put off the shame.
Then lest my life be cropped to keep you clear,
By flight I'll shun the danger that I fear.

It is obvious that he possesses a secret which the guilty king cannot allow to live with him, but his reaction seems an extraordinary volte-face from the fearless heroism of his opening speech.

Returning to his own kingdom of Tyre, Pericles falls into a state of melancholy:

> Why should this change of thoughts,
> The sad companion, dull-eyed melancholy,
> Be my so used guest as not an hour
> In the day's glorious walk or peaceful night,
> The tomb where grief should sleep, can breed me quiet?
> Here pleasures court mine eyes, and mine eyes shun them,
> And danger, which I feared, is at Antioch,
> Whose arm seems far too short to hit me here:
> Yet neither pleasure's art can joy my spirits,
> Nor yet the other's distance comfort me.
> Then it is thus: the passions of the mind,
> That have their first conception by misdread,
> Have after-nourishment and life by care;
> And what was first but fear what might be done,
> Grows elder now and cares it be not done.
> And so with me; the great Antiochus,
> 'Gainst whom I am too little to contend,
> Since he's so great can make his will his act,
> Will think me speaking, though I swear to silence;
> . . . . . . . . . . . . . . . . . . . . . . . . . . . . . .
> With hostile forces he'll o'erspread the land,
> And with th' ostent of war will look so huge,
> Amazement shall drive courage from the state,
> Our men be vanquished ere they do resist,
> And subjects punished that ne'er thought offence:
> Which care of them, not pity of myself,—
> Who am no more but as the tops of trees
> Which fence the roots they grow by and defend them,—
> Makes both my body pine and soul to languish,
> And punish that before that he would punish.

The depressive symptoms are revealed: Sleeplessness, loss of interest and concentration, suicidal thoughts—all are pathognomonic. The reasoning is not coherent. First, Antiochus is too far away to do any harm; then he will come with a vast army to destroy the princedom and its inhabitants. Pericles, who has already expressed his personal fear, now makes an obvious rationalization: he is not really concerned for himself, but for his princedom and his subjects.

What a downfall for the hero! Lawrence Babb ascribes his melancholy to his fear of Antiochus and, ostensibly, on factual and psychological evidence, this must be so. The sequence of progression from thought to action is commonly accepted as from perception through feeling: I see a lion—I feel afraid—I run away. But Pericles may be reacting according to the theory of Lange-James: I see a lion—I run away—therefore I feel afraid. Because he has taken flight he creates his melancholy fear.

But this is not acceptable dramatically. If there is any point in the conditional requirements for the status of tragic hero, physical fear is surely an absolute bar. Somerset Maugham has explored this situation in his story, *The Door of Opportunity*: his conclusion is that physical cowardice, admitted without shame, must turn from a man even the wife who dearly loves him. Although *Pericles* is not a tragedy, the structure of the drama of regeneration, peculiar to Shakespeare, makes the same demands on its hero. The fear and melancholy of Pericles must spring from some conflict deeper in the unconscious.

Pericles' next step is grossly illogical: he decides that he is not safe in Tyre, but must put to sea. How will this help his princedom and his subjects? In the Second World War ships were often safer away from port, but in the time of Pericles, with strategy dependent on fortification of a prepared position, such action is plainly ridiculous.

Nevertheless, Pericles is supported in his plan by his friend Helicanus, on whom the stamp of Horatio is evident. In offering to accept himself the cares and dangers of rule in Tyre, Helicanus is not merely humouring his Prince, but seems to understand that Pericles is in no fit mental state for his responsibilities. The sovereign remedy for melancholy—a long sea voyage—is once more to be applied.

The charm seems to work, because when Pericles arrives at Tarsus it is not as a refugee but in the guise of a deliverer. Thus he greets Cleon, Governor of famished Tarsus:

> Lord Governor, for so we hear you are;
> Let not our ships and number of our men
> Be like a beacon fired t' amaze your eyes.
> We have heard your miseries as far as Tyre,

And seen the desolation of your streets.

. . . . . . . . . . . . . . . . . . . . . .

And these our ships. . . . .
Are stored with corn to make your needy bread,
And give them life whom hunger starved half dead.

Away from Antiochus and Tyre, Pericles becomes restored to his heroic stature, producing a plausible rationalization for his visit, which was certainly not conceived originally for any advantage but his own.

But the restoration is brief. A letter from Helicanus reveals that Antiochus is on his track, and Pericles, like the Flying Dutchman, must pursue his restless course. A shipwreck is his next experience, to which his reaction shows that although he flees from Antiochus he is not afraid of death itself:

Yet cease your ire, you angry stars of heaven!

. . . . . . . . . . . . . . . . . . . . . .

Let it suffice the greatness of your powers
To have bereft a prince of all his fortunes;
And having thrown him from your wat'ry grave,
Here to have death in peace is all he'll crave.

Confirmation is soon provided that Pericles' physical courage has been restored. In the kingdom of Simonides, where he has been washed up, he enters a tourney of knights, emerging victorious to take the eye of the king's daughter, Thaisa. For her benefit he resumes his heroic pose: his shipwreck was whilst "looking for adventures in the world". But Simonides observes his underlying melancholy; well pleased that Pericles should wed Thaisa, he has the perception to bring him to the point by a stratagem. His angry accusation that his daughter has been bewitched is met by indignant protest, leading to ready capitulation when Simonides suddenly throws her at his head, making the decision himself—he has no mind to be left with a Hamlet on his hands.

We are given no time to observe whether marriage can finally dispel Pericles' melancholy. News comes that Antiochus and his daughter are dead; there is popular clamour in Tyre for the return of her prince. On the voyage, again accompanied by storm, Thaisa gives birth to a daughter and appears to die. To appease the storm her body is cast into the sea with somewhat indecent haste, but in a coffin that is watertight and comfortably lined.

The apparent death of Thaisa and her resuscitation, although not directly related to the character of Pericles, are of interest in consideration of the various types of stupor—a condition which he himself is later to experience.

There are four main varieties of stupor: toxic, depressive, schizoid and hysterical. In Thaisa's case we may presume that the stupor is of toxic origin, arising from physical causes after childbirth in unfavourable conditions. The response to treatment by the trained physician, Cerimon, confirms the diagnosis.

Pericles, with little show of grief for Thaisa, makes for Tarsus, presumably the nearest land, where he stays for a year with his infant daughter, Marina. Why he delays his own return to Tyre is not made clear, nor why he could not take the year-old child with him on his departure. He hands her over to King Cleon and his wife, Dionyza, for her further upbringing; this done he retires for the customary fourth-Act rest of the Shakespearian hero.

The next appearance of Pericles is in dumb-show. The time is fourteen years later, and Marina is believed to be dead. The stage directions read:

> Enter Pericles at one door with all his train, Cleon and Dionyza at the other. Cleon shows Pericles the tomb, whereat Pericles makes lamentation, puts on sackcloth, and in a mighty passion departs. . . .

According to the Chorus he:

> . . . in sorrow all devoured,
> With sighs shot through and biggest tears o'ershowered,
> Leaves Tarsus and again embarks. He swears
> Never to wash his face, nor cut his hairs:
> He puts on sackcloth, and to sea. . . .

It seems to have been forgotten that Pericles had already made a vow not to cut his hair when he left Marina fourteen years before!

After yet another storm at sea, the details of which we are mercifully spared, Pericles arrives at the coast of Mytilene, where by chance Marina dwells, in the esteem of all, having escaped the machinations of the Lady Macbeth-like Dionyza. She has converted the frequenters of the brothel where she has been deposited, by her chaste refusal of their advances—and in particular those of Lysimachus, Governor of Mytilene.

Lysimachus boards the Tyrian vessel, where he is addressed by the faithful Helicanus:

> Our vessel is of Tyre, in it the King;
> A man who for this three months hath not spoken
> To anyone, not taken sustenance
> But to prorogue his grief.

To Helicanus there is something more complex in the illness of Pericles than mere sorrow for his daughter's death. The cause:

> 'Twould be too tedious to repeat;
> But the main grief springs from the loss
> Of a beloved daughter and a wife.

The opinion of so loyal a character about his master is to be noted as we would that of Horatio about Hamlet.

Helicanus continues, with some ambiguity:

> . . . This was a goodly person
> Till the disaster that one mortal night,
> Drove him to this.

Pericles has experienced many disasters, but Helicanus seems to be referring to the original shipwreck in which he lost Thaisa, implying that he has never been normal since that time. Unfortunately we miss a more detailed statement from Helicanus through the premature arrival of Marina. Lysimachus urges:

> . . . Yet once more
> Let me entreat to know at large the cause
> Of your King's sorrow.

Helicanus replies:

> Sit, sir, I will recount it to you.
> But see, I am prevented.

Perhaps in this way we are spared the tedium of hearing again much that we already know, but there still remains the blank of fourteen years during which Pericles has ruled in Tyre. It would be interesting to hear what Helicanus has to say about this period.

Marina's treatment of Pericles is a blend of Elizabethan and modern psychotherapy. First she sings to him, a procedure recommended by Robert Burton. Using her music as a modern psychiatrist uses his pentothal she encourages him to speak of his misfortunes by comparing them with her own:

> . . . She speaks
> My lord, that, may be, hath endured a grief
> Might equal yours, if both were justly weighed.

She thus leads gently to a recognition derived from Greek
tragedy, a "discovery" of the kind defined by Aristotle as from
"sudden memory":

> Though wayward fortune did malign my state,
> My derivation was from ancestors
> Who stood equivalent with mighty kings:
> But time hath rooted out my parentage,
> And to the world and awkward casualties
> Bound me in servitude . . .

Recollection flickers in Pericles:

> My fortunes—parentage—good parentage—
> To equal mine! Was it not thus? What say you?

Naturally he cannot recognize Marina, whom he has not seen
since her infancy, but he notes the likeness to Thaisa:

> I am great with woe, and shall deliver weeping.
> My dearest wife was like this maid, and such a one
> My daughter might have been. . . .

Recognition still proceeds slowly. Even when Marina gives her
name Pericles is not convinced; he must be satisfied down to the
last detail. Later he projects these doubts on to Helicanus, who
has scarcely spoken:

> Give me my robes. I am wild in my beholding.
> O heavens bless my girl! But, hark, what music?
> Tell Helicanus, my Marina, tell him
> O'er, point by point, for yet he seems to doubt,
> How sure you are my daughter. But, what music?

At this point Pericles becomes hallucinated: he hears the "music
of the spheres", a private revelation, not given to Lysimachus or
Helicanus.

Later, falling asleep, Pericles sees Diana in a vision, who bids
him repair to Ephesus. There he is reunited with Thaisa; but
again recognition is slow, and he appears sceptical. When
Cerimon speaks of the jewels he found in the coffin he asks to
see them. The final proof comes from a ring given to him by
Simonides—a "discovery" by token, considered by Aristotle to
be weak.

The reunion of husband, wife and daughter draws from Shakespeare some of his noblest imagery. Pericles exclaims:

> This, this! No more, you gods! Your present kindness
> Makes my past miseries sports. You shall do well,
> That on the touching of her lips I may
> Melt, and no more be seen. O, come, be buried
> A second time within these arms.

Marina follows with:

> My heart
> Leaps to be gone into my mother's bosom.

The symbolism of this physical wholeness has a mystical, almost religious significance, which I regard as the key to the play.

I have taken the course of tracing the main events in the story with little passing comment, because the task of knitting these episodes into a coherent whole cannot be attempted until the complete sequence has been presented. It is accounted a defect in *Pericles* that the construction is episodic—far removed from Aristotelian principles—but, regardless of the authorship, I think that the form which this play takes is dictated by the nature of Pericles himself.

On first acquaintance with *Pericles* I received a distinct impression of a schizophrenic content, and the only production I have seen, at Stratford in 1958, strongly supported my original conclusion.

Fundamentally the play is about incest, a vice particularly common among schizophrenics. Whether he wrote the first part of *Pericles* or not, Shakespeare accepted the early situation as he found it, developing the character with complete fidelity therefrom.

The alarm and despondency experienced by Pericles after solving the riddle bears all the stigmata of spiritual rather than physical fear. We revolt most from those evils which we might be tempted to, and although Pericles is under no such temptation at the beginning of the play, the sex nausea which afflicts him can only be purged by the avowed and tested purity of his own daughter when she grows up.

It is natural that we should speculate about the relations between Shakespeare and the women of his own family; Frank Harris has indulged in this exhaustively, drawing a round condemnation from G. W. G. Wickham in his introduction to

*The London Shakespeare.* We know the ages of Shakespeare's two daughters, in their twenties when he was writing his final plays, so concerned with father-daughter relationships. We do not know how often he visited Stratford before his final retirement, but it may well be that a sudden awareness of the femininity of his newly grown-up daughters, with the need to establish a new relationship, contributed something to the writing of *Pericles*, of which the author was not consciously apprised.

The conduct of Pericles after the revelation of the incestuous relationship between Antiochus and his daughter is ill-considered and irrational. The emotional expression is not appropriate to the circumstances, and the action of flight does not become a man of expressed nobility and valour. Unconsciously Pericles is flying, not from Antiochus, but from himself. His evasions and rationalizations of the reason for his voyages show a personality tending to disintegrate from the shock of discovering that he has come near to the physical sharing of a woman with her father. This results in the "sex-nausea" which Dover Wilson finds in Shakespeare himself at this period: Pericles could not bring himself to woo Thaisa, and, intuitively, Simonides has to act as *deus ex machina*.

The death of Thaisa has no profound effect upon Pericles, because his libido instantly fixes itself upon his daughter. So long as she is a child he feels no guilt attached to this, although we have the evidence of Helicanus that he never resumed his normal self after the second shipwreck. Busy in his own kingdom for fourteen years, Pericles never saw his daughter nor took any step to bring her to him. His extravagant behaviour on learning of her death does not therefore seem natural in terms of actual loss; there must be some deeper psychological conflict. Pericles is unconsciously afraid that the sight of the nubile Marina will arouse in him the feelings of Antiochus for his daughter. Because he is afraid of this he has wished her dead—and his wish has been fulfilled: hence the overwhelming impact of shame and remorse.

The type of stupor must be inferred. My opinion is that it is catatonic—not depressive or hysterical, but in the absence of any detailed observations in the text this reading is rather from my conception of the character and motivation of Pericles than from direct clinical data.

The character of Marina as shown in the brothel scenes is of primary importance. Pericles has found that the flesh is impure; his faith, indeed his soul, can only be revived by the absolute purity of Marina. Thornton Wilder, in *The Skin of Our Teeth*, is a modern dramatist who has made the same point: to the father his daughter must be perfect. This is not a necessity particular to the plays concerned, but a psychological truth governing the relationship between fathers and their daughters at all times. The cliché of Victorian melodrama—"Never darken my door again!"—was based on sound psychological principles.

Marina's purity, although revealed to the audience, must be accepted intuitively by Pericles. But something further is needed before he can be restored to full mental health. Marina can arouse him from his stupor, but he is not yet normal. As evidence of his persisting schizophrenic state I adduce his auditory hallucinations—music heard by himself alone, and then the voice of Diana directing him to Ephesus. It is true that schizophrenic hallucinations do not normally serve to lead the patient to his salvation, but the symbolism of the final reunion admits of no other interpretation.

With the restoration of Thaisa, father and mother, husband and wife, father and daughter, mother and daughter—all are of one flesh, together in purity. Symbolically the union is also that of Pericles' divided personality—the separate parts come together at last in psychic harmony.

In Jungian terms Pericles is a restless intuitive extravert, with complementary, unconscious, introverted sensation. This type, according to Jung: "has a keen nose for things in the bud pregnant with future promise. He can never exist in stable, long-established conditions of generally acknowledged though limited value: because his eye is constantly ranging for new possibilities, stable conditions have an air of impending suffocation. He seizes hold of new objects and new ways with eager intensity, sometimes with extraordinary enthusiasm, only to abandon them cold-bloodedly, without regard and apparently without remembrance, as soon as their range becomes clearly defined and a promise of any considerable future development no longer clings to them. As long as a possibility exists, the intuitive is bound to it with thongs of fate. It is as though his whole life went out into the new situation. One gets the impression, which he himself shares, that he has just reached the definitive turning point in his life, and that from now on nothing else can seriously engage his thought and feeling. However reasonable and opportune it may be, and although every reasonable argument speaks in favour of stability, a day will come when nothing will deter him from regarding as a prison, the self-same situation that seemed to promise freedom and deliverance, and from acting accordingly. Neither reason nor feeling can restrain or discourage him from a new possibility, even though it may run counter to convictions hitherto unquestioned. Thinking and feeling, the indispensable components of conviction, are, with him, inferior functions, possessing no decisive weight; hence they lack the power to offer any lasting resistance to the force of intuition. And yet these are the only functions that are capable of creating any effectual compensation to the supremacy of intuition, since they can provide the intuitive with that judgment in which his type is altogether lacking . . ."

"This attitude has immense dangers—all too easily the intuitive may squander his life. He spends himself animating men and things, spreading around him an abundance of life—a life, however, which others live, not he. Were he able to rest with the actual thing, he would gather the fruit of his labours; yet all too soon must he be running after some fresh possibility, quitting his newly planted field, while others reap the harvest. In the end he goes empty away. But when the intuitive lets things reach such a pitch, he also has the unconscious against him. The unconscious of the intuitive has a certain similarity with that of the sensation-type. Thinking and feeling, being relatively repressed, produce infantile and archaic thoughts and feelings in the unconscious which may be compared with those of the counter-type. They likewise come to the surface in the form of intensive projections, and are just as absurd as those of the sensation-type, only to my mind they lack the other's mystical character; they are chiefly concerned with quasi-actual things, in the nature of sexual, financial, and other hazards, as, for instance, suspicions of approaching illness. . . . He rids himself of the restrictions of reason, only to fall a victim to unconscious neurotic compulsions in the form of over-subtle, negative reasoning, hair-splitting dialectics, and a compulsive tie to the sensation of the object. His conscious attitude, both to the sensation and the sensed object, is one of sovereign superiority and disregard.

Not that he means to be inconsiderate or superior—he simply does not see the object that everyone else sees; his oblivion is similar to that of the sensation-type—only, with the latter, the soul of the object is missed. For this oblivion the object sooner or later takes revenge in the form of hypochondriacal, compulsive ideas, phobias, and every imaginable kind of absurd bodily sensation."

In the case of Pericles, the psychological trauma at Antioch breeds war between the conscious and unconscious elements in his personality, allowing sensations of a primitive kind to make alarming raids into consciousness. Not until he can form a right relationship with his anima, a conjunction of the personalities of Thaisa and Marina, can his psyche become fully mature.

John Vyvyan describes the sequence of regeneration in Shakespeare's later plays as follows:

1. A soul is shown containing the principles of strength which will enable it to pass the test.
2. The voices of the higher self which will enable it to pass the test are shown.
3. There is a temptation scene, and the hero triumphs, because he is true to the self and faithful to love.
4. There is a confirmatory experience, tending towards inner sovereignty and lordship of the soul.
5. and 6. A second test and a second confirmation.
7. The act of creative mercy, including self-forgiveness.
8. The experience of enlightenment.
9. The symbolic union of love.

I find it hard to apply this sequence to *Pericles*. The first exposition of character is belied by his reaction to the revelation of the riddle, which is presumably the first temptation. But what is Pericles tempted to? If it is to marry a tainted bride, Antiochus is the arbiter of that. If it is his courage which is in question he does not pass the test. And in all that ensues between this scene and the final regeneration I can find little evidence of any tendency towards inner sovereignty. The experience of enlightenment and the symbolic union of love I accept without question, but I prefer to fit the general structure of the play into the simpler five Act pattern of the tragedies, among which an alternative last Act could well have placed it.

This is how I visualize the structure:

In Act I we see an inexperienced but essentially noble character faced with an appalling discovery about sex.

In Act II his reaction to this discovery is shown: he runs away from its implications.

In Act III his flight is halted by marriage, but his problem is unsolved, leading to a fresh crisis through the loss of his wife and the abandonment of his child.

In Act IV the protagonist is off the stage whilst we observe the forces of regeneration unfolding in his daughter Marina, comparable to the assembly of the forces of retribution in the fourth Act of *Macbeth*.

In Act V Pericles' sex-nausea is overcome by the purity of Marina, bringing the family together in the symbolic union of love.

In the view of Ulrici the plot of *Pericles* is held together by a single idea—the quest for, loss of and recovery of genuine love. I agree with this, but emphasize that the love of a father for his daughter is the problem which engages Pericles throughout.

Shakespeare's delicacy of feeling forbids him to give a name to the daughter of Antiochus—incest is the "nameless vice". In his short play *The Purification* Tennessee Williams makes the same point by the urging of the guilty brother that his sister "had no name".

# 10

## LEONTES—THE PARANOID

ALTHOUGH not suffering from a depressive illness as understood in modern terminology, Leontes presents a typical example of the jealous melancholy described by Elizabethan writers.

There is nearly as much critical literature of *The Winter's Tale* as there is of *Hamlet*, but there is less illumination of the character of Leontes in the text.

The first enlightenment comes from Camillo, adjudged by John Vyvyan to represent Fidelity in the play, comparable to Polonius in *Hamlet*, Escalus in *Measure for Measure* and Gonzalo in *The Tempest*. Whilst agreeing that fidelity is his important quality, I prefer to equate Camillo, like Helicanus, with Horatio, particularly in considering the validity of his opinions about his master.

Camillo has this to say about the relations between Leontes and Polixenes:

> Sicilia cannot show himself over-kind to Bohemia. They were trained together in their childhoods; and there rooted between them such an affection, which cannot choose but branch now. Since their more mature dignities and royal necessities made separation of their society, their encounters, though not personal, hath been royally attorneyed with interchange of gifts, letters, loving embassies; that they have seemed to be together, though absent, shook hands as over a vast; and embraced, as it were, from the ends of opposite winds. The heavens continue their loves!

When Polixenes wishes to return to Bohemia, Leontes urges him to stay with an insistence beyond mere hospitable politeness. Polixenes is obdurate until Hermione adds a humorous threat that the reluctant guest must be forcibly detained. Having won his acceptance, she says she will be:

> Not your gaoler then,
> But your kind hostess. Come, I'll question you
> Of my lord's tricks and yours when you were boys.
> You were pretty lordlings then?

To which Polixenes replies:

> We were, fair Queen,
> Two lads that thought there was no more behind
> But such a day tomorrow as today,
> And to be boy eternal. . . .
> We were as twinned lambs that did frisk i' th' sun,
> And bleat the one at th' other. What we changed
> Was innocence for innocence; we knew not
> The doctrine of ill-doing, nor dreamed
> That any did. Had we pursued that life,
> And our weak spirits ne'er been higher reared
> With stronger blood, we should have answered heaven
> Boldly "Not guilty"; the imposition cleared
> Hereditary ours.

This description of carefree pre-adolescence was possibly in the mind of Sir Compton Mackenzie when writing a chapter in his book *Sinister Street*, entitled "Boyhood's Glory".

The critics are in doubt whether the last phrase implies that the boys were blameless but for their inescapable quota of original sin, or had, by their innocence, overcome even that. The meaning of the whole passage is dependent on the tone of Hermione's query, made immediately the prolongation of the visit has been settled. Polixenes seems to be on the defensive, assuring Hermione of the innocence of this early friendship by an over-protestation. I think it important that undertones of jealousy are first apparent in Hermione, revealing that the boyhood friendship of Leontes and Polixenes is the mainspring of the situation.

Leontes' jealous outburst is all the more abrupt, coming as it does hard upon the urgency of his invitation. Hermione has only to offer Polixenes her hand—and the spark is ignited:

> LEONTES (*aside*):          Too hot, too hot!
> To mingle friendship far is mingling bloods.
> I have tremor cordis on me: my heart dances,
> But not for joy; not joy. This entertainment
> May a free face put on, derive a liberty
> From heartiness, from bounty, fertile bosom,

And well become the agent; 't may, I grant;
But to be paddling palms and pinching fingers,
As now they are, and making practised smiles,
As in a looking-glass, and then to sigh, as 'twere
The mort o' th' deer:—O, that is an entertainment
My bosom likes not, nor my brows! . . .

The simile of "The mort o' the' deer" symbolizes well the contest between two men for one woman, like stags fighting for mastery over the hind.

In his next speech Leontes introduces a retrospective jealousy. Gazing at Mamillius the incredible thought strikes him that he may not be his own son. As yet he is midway between an obsession and a delusion—still struggling to obey what reason tells him, but impelled to listen to the voice of feeling rising from the unconscious. This feeling is known in modern psychological terms as the "affect", clearly understood by Shakespeare in the same sense, except that he uses the longer form:

Affection, thy intention stabs the centre:
Thou dost make possible things not so held,
Communicat'st with dreams;—how can this be?
With what's unreal thou coactive art,
And fellow'st nothing. Then 'tis very credent
Thou may'st co-join with something; and thou dost,
And that beyond commission, and I find it,
And that to the infection of my brains
And hard'ning of my brows.

The *New London Shakespeare* cites Hudson as dismissing this passage as deliberately unintelligible; to the psychiatrist it is perhaps the most remarkable that Shakespeare ever wrote. Given the clue that "affection" is the same as the "affect" every word falls neatly into place. Early commentators have been puzzled because they took "affection" to mean imagination, whilst Furness and his successors have missed the meaning through trying to reconcile it with the normal use of the word in the sense of "fondness". I am sure that Leontes is invoking feeling as opposed to reason; the passage may then be paraphrased thus:

Feeling—this is the clue to my problem:
It can contradict the force of reason,
Its language is that of dreams [i.e. proceeding from the unconscious]. How does it operate?

It denies what the conscious holds as true,
Creating its own facts without logical foundation.
But it is obvious
That it must then adapt the outside world to its own autonomy.
   This it does,
In a manner beyond my conscious control, which affects me
By destroying my ability to reason,
And compelling me to the physical expression of my jealousy in
   my features.

As at the opening of *The Merchant of Venice*, but in the far more subtle language of the mature Shakespeare, we have a brilliant exposition of the basis of a mental disease—in this case paranoia. This outpouring is, of course, from the unconscious mind of Leontes: the paranoid has no insight. The obscurity of the language prevents Leontes himself from bringing his reason in opposition to the unconscious force of feeling which is overwhelming him.

It is not surprising that critics with no experience of psychiatry have found this passage difficult; but it is useless to object that Shakespeare could not himself have had such precocious knowledge either. It is all there, and what is more astonishing is that so much understanding of morbid psychology has been packed into so few words—and in a poetic metre.

Now controlled by his suspicions, Leontes takes action. To convince the reluctant Camillo of Hermione's guilt he pours out a catalogue of evidence derived from his own imagination:

                    Is whispering nothing?
Is leaning cheek to cheek? Is meeting noses?
Kissing with inside lip? Stopping the career
Of laughter with a sigh?—a note infallible
Of breaking honesty;—horsing foot on foot?
Skulking in corners? Wishing clocks more swift?
Hours, minutes? noon, midnight? and all eyes
Blind with the pin and web but theirs, theirs only,
That would unseen be wicked? Is this nothing?
Why, then the world and all that's in't is nothing;
The covering sky is nothing; Bohemia nothing;
My wife is nothing; nor nothing have these nothings,
If this be nothing.

In the few moments during which Leontes has observed Polixenes and Hermione together they could hardly have had the opportunity for all the misconduct complained of, nor

would they have communicated to him their views on the passage
of time.

To Camillo, as to us, these accusations are the result of a
"diseased opinion". Torn between loyalty to his master and his
conviction of the Queen's innocence, he reluctantly agrees to
poison Polixenes, provided that Leontes will afterwards be
reconciled to Hermione. But his resolution does not long survive his next encounter with Polixenes. Although confessedly
"charged in honour and by him I think honourable", he quickly
betrays his instructions to his victim and engineers his escape.
In this action, although untrue to his master, he keeps faith
with his own conscience and is therefore secure in his character
of Fidelity.

Unnecessary emphasis seems to have been laid on Camillo's
possession of "the keys of all the posterns". When Leontes asks
how they "came so easily open", he is reminded by the First
Lord that it was:

> By his great authority, (Camillo's)
> Which often hath no less prevailed than so
> On your command.

It has been suggested that the posterns might have been the
avenue for the admission of mistresses to Leontes, thus accounting for a sense of guilt projected by him on to Hermione—and
the origin of his own morbid jealousy. S. L. Bethell considers it
more probable that a secret ingress for diplomatic messengers was
concerned. But I do not take the First Lord's reply to mean that
it was a common practice for Camillo to open the posterns; he is
expressing his general mistrust and jealousy of the excessive
authority with which Camillo has been invested by Leontes,
illustrating Shakespeare's habit of giving even to minor characters some personal expression of feeling about the events in
which they are concerned.

In his abuse of the truant Camillo, Leontes gives vent to the
usual ideas of reference in the paranoid, by accusing him of
prior implication in the adulterous plot between Hermione and
Polixenes. Robbed of his intended victim, he despatches the
Queen to prison, heedless of the fervent reproaches of his entourage. To satisfy them he decides to consult the Delphic
Oracle, confident of the answer he will receive.

In prison Hermione gives birth to a daughter. In a despairing attempt to move Leontes to compassion, Paulina—of whom more later—brings in the newborn child. Despite the resemblance to himself Leontes remains convinced that Polixenes is the father; he will relent only so far as to permit for the infant banishment to some unfriendly shore, there to take its chance against nature and the elements.

In the next scene Hermione is placed on trial and the verdict of the Oracle is given:

> Hermione is chaste; Polixenes blameless; Camillo a true subject; Leontes a jealous tyrant; his innocent babe truly begotten; and the King shall live without an heir, if that which is lost be not found.

The reaction of Leontes is immediate:

> There is no truth at all i' th' oracle!

This is the final demonstration, if any were needed, that Leontes is suffering from a delusion in the modern definition—a false belief persisting in spite of all proof to the contrary. To a Greek of the time the Delphic Oracle was infallible, and its message may be regarded as definite proof.

Although the intellectual appeal of the Oracle cannot reverse an emotionally activated belief, a shock profoundly felt can succeed where reason has failed. Stunned by the shame accorded to his mother, Leontes' son, Mamillius, is dead.

Leontes repents at once:

> Apollo's angry; and the heavens themselves
> Do strike at my injustice.

But he is more concerned to reconcile himself to Apollo than to his maltreated Queen, who has fainted at the news. When Paulina bids him:

> Look down
> And see what death is doing

his concern is almost callous:

> Take her hence.
> Her heart is but o'ercharged; she will recover.

He then softens a little:

> I have too much believed mine own suspicion.
> Beseech you, tenderly apply to her
> Some remedies for life.

But his preoccupation is not with Hermione:

> Apollo, pardon
> My great profaneness 'gainst thine oracle!
> I'll reconcile me to Polixenes;
> New woo my Queen; recall good Camillo,
> Whom I proclaim a man of truth, of mercy;
> For, being transported by my jealousies
> To bloody thoughts and to revenge, I chose
> Camillo for the minister to poison
> My friend Polixenes; which had been done
> But that the mind of good Camillo tardied
> My swift command, though I with death and with
> Reward did threaten and encourage him,
> Not doing it and being done. He, most humane
> And filled with honour, to my kingly guest
> Unclasped my practice, quit his fortunes here,
> Which you knew great, and to the hazard
> Of all uncertainties himself commended,
> No richer than his honour. How he glisters
> Through my rust. And how his piety
> Does my deeds make the blacker!

In this speech of newly dawned repentance Hermione is mentioned only in one half-line; all the contrition is directed to Polixenes and Camillo. Paulina is swift to remind Leontes of the greatest injury:

> That thou betrayedst Polixenes, 'twas nothing;
> That did but show thee, of a fool, inconstant
> And damnable ingrateful. Nor was't much,
> Thou wouldst have poisoned good Camillo's honour,
> To have him kill a king; poor trespasses,
> More monstrous standing by: whereof I reckon
> The casting forth to crows thy baby daughter
> To be or none or little, though a devil
> Would have shed water out of fire ere done't:
> Nor is't directly laid to thee, the death
> Of the young prince, whose honourable thoughts,
> Thoughts high for one so tender, cleft the heart
> That could conceive a gross and foolish sire
> Blemished his gracious dam. This is not, no,
> Laid to thy answer; but the last,—O lords,
> When I have said, cry "woe!"—the Queen, the Queen,
> The sweet'st, dear'st creature's dead, and vengeance for't
> Not dropped down yet.

Paulina, in this speech—and at other times—expresses our own view of the situation. She has no place in the plot other than that of *deus ex machina* in the final Act, and may be regarded as a chorus figure whose comments are those of the author. There is no character quite like her in all Shakespeare's plays. She is the only female to perform the function of chorus, and though she remains outside the plot until the end, her feelings are at all times deeply involved; she is not the detached observer represented by a Jaques or Feste in the main. The character has, I believe, a deeper significance which I will discuss later.

Shakespeare gives few words to Leontes for expressing his realization that his delusion has brought about the death of Hermione; the simplicity of his grief is in moving contrast to the rhetoric of his past utterances:

> Go on, go on!
> Thou canst not speak too much: I have deserved
> All tongues to talk their bitt'rest.

Paulina is moved to regret her outspokenness, but Leontes checks her:

> Thou dist speak but well
> When most the truth; which I receive much better
> Than to be pitied of thee. Prithee, bring me
> To the dead bodies of my Queen and son.
> One grace shall be for both: upon them shall
> The causes of their death appear, unto
> Our shame perpetual. Once a day I'll visit
> The chapel where they lie, and tears shed there
> Shall be my recreation. So long as nature
> Will bear up with this exercise, so long
> I daily vow to use it. Come and lead me
> To these sorrows.

And here the play might well end, complete in itself as a tragedy. What follows is something original and unique. Wilson Knight reminds us that the resurrection and reunion plots of *Pericles*, *The Winter's Tale* and *The Tempest* stand alone in English literature.

The absence of the protagonist throughout Act IV is in accordance with Shakespeare's normal practice, but the transition in *The Winter's Tale* is abrupt and contrary to all the unities. Time moves forward sixteen years, with a shift of scene from a plausible Sicily to an unlikely Bohemia (with a coast-line!), and of mood from tragical to pastoral.

The new plot concerns the love between Florizel, son of the maligned Polixenes, and Perdita, abandoned daughter of Leontes, who has been brought up as a shepherdess. The wooing of Perdita by Florizel is a simple love story of fairy-tale quality, with no apparent affinity to the earlier part of the play and little presage of the events to come. Only Polixenes perceives that:

> Nothing she does or seems
> But smacks of something greater than herself,
> Too noble for this place.

Like Ophelia, Perdita expresses her inmost thoughts with flowers; but the gifts to Polixenes and Camillo of rosemary and rue seem to indicate nothing more than the "grace and remembrance" which accompanies them as her courteous welcome. It will be recalled that, in *Hamlet*, rosemary is for remembrance and rue may be called "herb of grace o' Sundays".

The important flower in Perdita's catalogue is the "gillivor". To Perdita natural simplicity and purity are all-important: gillyflowers are streaked—"which some call nature's bastards" —therefore she will none of them:

> For I have heard it said
> There is an art which in their piedness shares
> With great creating nature.

There is some dramatic irony in Polixenes' defence of art wedded to nature:

> You see, sweet maid, we marry
> A gentler scion to the wildest stock,
> And make conceive a bark of baser kind
> By bud of nobler race.

This is exactly what he refuses to countenance later when he learns of Florizel's desire to marry the shepherdess.

Perdita is adamant in her rejection of the gillyflower. She'll not put:

> The dibble in earth to set one slip of them;
> No more than were I painted I would wish
> This youth should say 'twere well, and only therefore
> Desire to breed by me.

Her love must be pure and natural, with no meretricious aids.

This, added to Hamlet's violent condemnation of these artifices in women, suggests that Shakespeare did not much care for sophistication.

Perdita would conjure up flowers symbolic of the spring in its virginity; then, as in Whitsuntide pastorals, strew lilies "like a bank for love to lie and play on"—the apotheosis of pure romantic love. In the same mood, Florizel would have Perdita sing and dance eternally—"and own no other function". Later he tells Polixenes:

> . . . were I crowned the most imperial monarch,
> Thereof most worthy, were I the fairest youth
> That ever made eye swerve, had force and knowledge
> More than was ever man's, I would not prize them
> Without her love; for her employ them all;
> Commend them and condemn them to her service
> Or to their own perdition.

This is heroic love, matched by Perdita's self-denial. When she realizes that her love might cost Florizel a kingdom, her renunciation is instant:

> Will't please you, sir, begone?
> I told you what would come of this. Beseech you,
> Of your own state take care. This dream of mine,—
> Being now awake, I'll queen it no inch farther,
> But milk my ewes and weep.

Florizel is steadfast:

> Not for Bohemia, nor the pomp that may
> Be thereat gleaned; for all the sun sees, or
> The close earth wombs, or the profound seas hide
> In unknown fathoms, will I break my oath
> To this my fair beloved.

As Camillo helped Polixenes to escape from the wrath of his master, Leontes, so now he plans to restore to her still grieving father the daughter who is now assailed by the wrath of his new master, Polixenes.

After sixteen years Leontes is still beset by the reproaches of Paulina, who hammers at his memory with the image of the wife he has lost, bidding him not marry again except with her own express permission. No doubt the death of her husband, Antigonus, on Leontes' errand, has added a few barbs to her tongue; I think we may agree that sixteen years of Paulina must have proved a heavy penance.

When Florizel and Perdita arrive there is no joyful reunion between father and daughter, as in *Pericles*. The "discovery", related by other characters, would be regarded by Aristotle as weak. But Shakespeare's purpose is different in the two plays. In *Pericles* the father-daughter relationship is the most important from the first; whereas, in *The Winter's Tale*, Perdita is a symbol of her mother and important to the plot only in this respect. A scene of recognition between Leontes and Perdita would have gravely weakened the final *coup de théâtre*.

The resurrection of Hermione is of one who has lived and aged in the normal way—she is no Sleeping Beauty who has survived the passage of the years unchanged. Leontes is surprised to see the statue more wrinkled than the Hermione he knew; Paulina hastily ascribes this to the sculptor's art. It is surely clear that Hermione has neither died nor been in a cataleptic trance, but has been looked after, and presumably fed, by Paulina for all these years.

In her one speech after the "resurrection", Hermione, whether deliberately or not, gives the game away. She says to Perdita:

> For thou shalt hear that I,
> Knowing by Paulina that the oracle
> Gave hope thou wast in being, have preserved
> Myself to see the issue.

This must refer to some later consultation of Delphi, because Hermione was present on the original occasion when the oracle promised that "the King shall live without an heir, if that which is lost be not found". There would be no need for Paulina to inform her of a message which she had already heard: the presumption is that she has all the time been in touch with a fully conscious and cognizant Queen.

Paulina has a final thrust at Leontes, reminding him that, in contrast to his own new-found happiness, she herself is left as an "old turtle" without her mate. Possibly to rid himself finally of her reproaches, Leontes insists that she should marry Camillo—a somewhat ambiguous reward for his fidelity.

In this summary of the plot of *The Winter's Tale*, in so far as it is relevant to the character of Leontes, I have restricted quotation to what is necessary for my purpose. I shall now consider in more detail Leontes' jealous melancholy which sets the plot in motion.

According to Kenneth Muir the primary source of the play is Greene's romance, *Pandosto*, published in 1588. In this work, Egistus (Polixenes) and Bellaria (Hermione) actually do become inseparable, although not guilty of adultery. It is Bellaria who appeals to the oracle, and Pandosto, recognizing its validity, repents at once. This is an important distinction, because it is the emotional impact of the death of Mamillius—not the intellectual appeal of the oracle—which first softens Leontes. Shakespeare, as is his wont, has created an intriguing psychological mystery by presenting an apparently unmotivated jealousy. J. I. M. Stewart does not regard this as dramatic ineptitude, but "a handling according to the laws of drama of little-recognized impulses and conflicts within the minds of the author and his audience". It is the purpose of this chapter to elucidate some of this material—*pace* E. M. Tillyard, who advises us to refrain from such an exercise.

There is no difficulty in diagnosing Leontes' mental condition either by Elizabethan or modern standards: he is suffering from a jealous melancholy, or paranoia. In this case Bradley's dictum that Shakespeare's portrayals of mental disease affect the character only and never the action of the play cannot possibly be sustained—the whole plot of *The Winter's Tale* is dependent on the insane suspicions of Leontes.

Burton considers jealousy to be a deformed branch of love melancholy. He says that if an ugly or deformed man marry a beautiful woman he is apt to be jealous, showing that there is nothing truly original in Adler's "organ inferiority" apart from the language. Burton's description of the symptoms corresponds with what might be read about paranoia in any textbook today. He allows that the prognosis is bad, proceeding from suspicion to hatred and so to frenzy—madness—injury—murder—and despair. In *The Winter's Tale* we can follow this series exactly; the procession from suspicion to injury is rapid, and the murder of Polixenes misfires, but the supposed death of Hermione is willed by Leontes—to be followed by sixteen years of despair.

Burton recommends diversion by occupation and company as the best treatment, and the arrangement of suitable marriages for prevention.

This is a convenient place to mention Shakespeare's other

jealous husbands. Lawrence Babb considers that Leontes and Othello are not naturally jealous—as is Ford, whereas Margaret Webster cites Ford as the precursor of Leontes in Shakespeare's mind. But surely Leontes stands alone as the husband whose jealousy is completely endogenous. Ford is deceived by the boasts of Falstaff, although too ready to believe them without thought of the utter unreliability of the character who makes them; this distinguishes his jealousy from that of Postumus and Othello, both of whom are deliberately misled by others—by Iachimo for gain and by Iago for gain and spite combined. Perhaps Othello's race acts as a kind of organ inferiority, making him more ready to credit Desdemona's infidelity with a man of her own colour. His jealousy is slowly brought to the boil by Iago's repeated insinuations, which creates more sympathy for him than for Postumus, deceived on the evidence of a bracelet alone—much as Claudio plans his revenge on Hero before he has any proof of Don John's accusation.

I see a potential Leontes rather in Orsino, married to a girl much younger than himself, and whose vacillating views of the constancy of love in men and women demonstrate an emotionally immature and unstable personality.

Modern psychiatry has little to add to Burton's description of jealous melancholy apart from the word "paranoia". The prognosis is notoriously bad, presenting the regeneration of Leontes as an exceptional problem.

It is not normally considered practical to go deeply into the unconscious motives which express themselves in paranoia. As the subject is not open to reason, psycho-analytic treatment can do no good, and indeed may do considerable harm by concentrating the patient's attention on his delusions when, as Burton suggests, the most hopeful line of treatment is by diverting him from them.

Nevertheless, Freud has propounded a theory of three layers of sexual jealousy, which Professor Stewart accepts as relevant to the case of Leontes. The first and most superficial type is normal competitive jealousy. At a deeper level there is jealousy from projection on to the sexual partner of guilt arising unconsciously from the subject's own infidelity. Deeper in the unconscious there are sexual urges causing jealousy displaced to the heterosexual partner from a homosexual attachment to the accused co-respondent. In this regard the delusions are an unconscious defence against a sexual attitude unacceptable to society. Professor Stewart regards the jealousy of Leontes as truly delusional, arising from the deepest layer; Arthur Sewell whilst agreeing that Leontes projects a sense of his own guilt on to Hermione, denies its specific nature.

If Freud's theory is accepted, there is no doubt that Leontes' jealousy is at the deepest level: it is plainly delusional. There is nothing in the text of the play to suggest infidelity on the part of Leontes himself or any heterosexual attachment giving grounds for guilt in this connection. I have already discounted the evidence of the opening of the posterns. On the other hand there is abundant reference to a deep attachment between Leontes and Polixenes. To avoid misunderstanding I must emphasize that there is no suggestion of overt homosexual conduct. As Shakespeare explains through the mouth of Polixenes, what they exchanged was "innocence for innocence". But though unconscious, the sexual element is there. Why should Hermione sound Polixenes so keenly on his boyhood friendship with her husband? The impression is of something that had always come between husband and wife. It is inconceivable that Leontes should break out so abruptly into his delusional system of thought unless his marriage had been for some time on the brink of disruption. That the reason for this should be unconscious to Leontes himself does not affect the argument; the lack of insight in the paranoid subject protects him from such revelations.

Freud, whether we agree with him or not, can take us no further than this—his psychological theory is redactive and does not point the way to any cure or regeneration. With Jung it is different. John Vyvyan uses his terminology to depict Bohemia as the world of the soul, surrounded by sea—the defence of the unconscious, suggesting that it may be Shakespeare's purpose, like a psycho-analyst, to show how the outer life may be recreated from within. For him, the love of Florizel and Perdita in the fourth Act symbolizes the regeneration of true love in Leontes; the deaths of Mamillius and Hermione act as a catharsis or shock treatment, conditioning him for the long process of spiritual rehabilitation. I prefer Wilson Knight's ascription of the shock to that of the death of Mamillius alone; the repentance begins before Hermione "dies", gathering no increased momentum from the second blow.

Arthur Sewell is surely mistaken in attributing the change in Leontes to the pronouncement of the oracle, which he instantly rejects, maintaining his ground until his feelings are shaken by the death of Mamillius.

John Vyvyan sees in Perdita, as in Hermione her mother, the pure and good anima archetype described by Jung, but has no comment to make about Paulina. Consideration of this character calls for a return to Freud, in whose system Paulina represents the super-ego. Outside her function as a chorus she has no independent existence, and may therefore be regarded as a symbolic figure, a part of Leontes. In simpler terms she stands for the voice of conscience, which cannot be stilled until Hermione returns to life. She also has a place in Jung's archetypal theory, in which she represents the helpful shadow, a more dynamic conception which fits her for the role of regenerator as well as accuser.

Before leaving Jung I must consider Leontes in relation to his basic psychological type. This is no easy matter, because we have so little indication of his personality before delusional fancies overwhelmed him. But I have no hesitation in labelling him as an extraverted sensation type, of which Shakespeare's most obvious example is Falstaff. At the risk of being accused of selective quotation in accordance with preconceived theory I must restrict myself to what in Jung's chapter seems most relevant:

"His aim (the sensation extravert's) is concrete enjoyment, and his morality is similarly orientated. . . . He is by no means unlovable; on the contrary, he frequently has a charming and lively capacity for enjoyment; he is sometimes a jolly fellow and often a refined aesthete. . . . When he 'senses', everything essential has been said and done. Nothing can be more than concrete and actual; conjectures that transcend or go beyond the concrete are only permitted on condition that they enhance sensation. . . . In so far as he thinks and feels, he always reduces down to objective foundations, i.e. to influences coming from the object, quite unperturbed by the most violent departures from logic. Tangible reality, under any conditions makes him breathe again. In this respect he is unexpectedly credulous. He will, without hesitation, relate an obvious psychogenic symptom to the falling barometer, while the existence of a psychic conflict seems to him a fantastic abnormality. . . . But the more sensation predominates, so that the sensing subject disappears behind the sensation, the more unsatisfactory does this type become. Either he develops into a crude pleasure-seeker or he becomes an unscrupulous, designing sybarite. Although the object is entirely indispensable to him, yet, as something existing in and through itself, it is none the less depreciated. It is ruthlessly violated and essentially ignored, since now its sole use is to stimulate sensation. The hold upon the object is pushed to the utmost limit. The unconscious is, accordingly, forced out of its *métier* as a compensatory function and driven into open opposition. But, above all, the repressed intuitions begin to assert themselves in the form of projections upon the object. The strangest conjectures arise; in the case of a sexual object, jealous phantasies and anxiety states play a great role. More acute cases develop every sort of phobia, and especially compulsive symptoms. The pathological contents have a remarkable air of unreality, with a frequent moral or religious colouring. . . . The whole culture of thought and feeling seems, in this second personality, to be twisted into a morbid primitiveness; reason is hair-splitting sophistry—morality is dreary moralizing and palpable Pharasaism—religion is absurd superstition—intuition, the noblest of human gifts, is a mere personal subtlety, a sniffing into every corner: instead of searching the horizon, it recedes to the narrowest gauge of human meanness. . . . When he becomes neurotic, he is much harder to treat in the rational way, because the functions to which the physician must appeal are in a relatively undifferentiated state; hence little or no trust can be placed in them. Special means of bringing emotional pressure to bear are often needed to make him at all conscious."

I think the above is a fair selection, of which the last sentence is particularly apposite in the case of Leontes.

The resurrection of Hermione, described by Wilson Knight as "the most strikingly conceived and profoundly penetrating moment in English Literature", is the subject of a wealth of commentary from philosophical, metaphysical and religious aspects. I regard this unique stroke as part of Shakespeare's genius for illustrating psychological truth. He knew well, either from observation or intuition, that there is no cure in this world for the paranoid state. Repentance and a change of heart cannot be brought about even by the most profound emotional shock—

this can only condition the patient for a temporary receptivity to more reasonable views. Hence the long lapse of sixteen years, during which Leontes must re-live his courtship of Hermione through the medium of Florizel and Perdita.

Modern critics are in agreement that the fourth Act of *The Winter's Tale* is a form of allegory. S. L. Bethell describes it as a "mythological kind of symbolism". Wilson Knight thinks that Shakespeare is emphasizing the quickening power of youth and its freedom from guilt, in some ways parallel to the imagery in Wordsworth's *Ode on Intimations of Immortality.* Stopford Brooke contrasts the bad passion which hurries Leontes into a world of death with the good passion which hurries Florizel into a world of life. E. M. Tillyard, on the same lines, regards the heroine as split into two persons—Hermione the real woman and Perdita the symbol.

All these opinions are complementary, not mutually exclusive. I think most emphasis should be laid on the failure of the love between Leontes and Hermione as contrasted with the idyllic love between Florizel and Perdita. Perdita's lines stress her virgin purity, with lilies to grace her marriage bed in token of this. But she will give up Florizel completely rather than cause him any hurt. Florizel puts his love for Perdita above all earthly ambition, even to the renunciation of a kingdom. If Leontes and Hermione had thus begun their courtship their union would not have reached the point at which it broke.

According to Stopford Brooke, Leontes is essentially noble, but weak. He regards his violence as a cover for this weakness, a trait shown also by Richard II. The sixteen years of repentance work the jealousy out of his nature. To me, the validity of the repentance of Leontes involves a conception of the courtship of Florizel and Perdita as a rebirth and reformation of his own early love for Hermione, lived through in the manner of a psycho-analytic redaction.

Many critics find a religious symbolism in the play. S. L. Bethell calls it a parable of the Christian religion, in which sin comes from without—not from the will of Leontes but from the Devil, thus explaining the apparent lack of motive for his jealousy. The last two Acts represent, to Bethell, purgatory and atonement, a viewpoint shared in general by Wilson Knight; whilst Tillyard goes so far as to say that "Shakespeare's attempt to compress into *The Winter's Tale* the mainly human theme of tragedy with the theme of planes of reality tending to the religious is almost as if he aimed at rendering the complete theme of Dante's *Divine Comedy*."

There is nothing incompatible between religious truth and psychological truth—indeed, for there to be any truth in either they must be inseparable. But I find some difficulty in accepting the lost sixteen years as a state of purgatory for Leontes. If it was Shakespeare's intention to depict this, why did he not show us the progression of repentance in Leontes? The main reason is probably in his scheme of dramatic construction, in which he diverts attention from his hero during the fourth Act of his plays, so that the actor can conserve his full dramatic powers for the later climax. Perhaps if we use the word "limbo" instead of purgatory for the state of suspense the religious and psychological points of view may come closer together.

In the last Act, some critics regard the reappearance of Hermione as a true resurrection from a prolonged state of suspended animation. From the text, it appears more indicated that she had been shielded by Paulina in voluntary seclusion until the repentance of Leontes should be fully assured—as evidenced by his agreement to remarry only with the consent of Paulina (i.e. according to his true conscience). If it were otherwise, an attractive theory could be put forward: that as the paranoia of Leontes cannot be cured in this world, he must join Hermione in the next to recreate his marriage. This involves the understanding that Hermione is truly dead and that his fantasy of her resurrection is at his own death-point, parallel with the dying fantasy in which Lear senses Cordelia's return to life. But I am afraid that the text will not allow of this.

Shakespeare, from his own observation, knew that the cure of paranoia required a miracle. I find this miracle, not in the resurrection of Hermione, but in the mystical regeneration of pure love in Leontes through the courtship of Florizel and Perdita.

# 11

## SHAKESPEARE AND HIS CHARACTERS

MANY theories have been put forward about the relationship of
Shakespeare's characters to himself and to individuals living in
his time; endeavours have also been made to link the moods of
his plays with events in his own life.

Shakespeare's life is surprisingly well documented. We know
the dates of his birth, marriage and death, and many facts about
his family. Contemporary references to him form the subject
matter of a commentary by C. M. Ingleby nearly a century ago,
now known as the *Shakespeare Allusion Book*. But many of the
things which are missing are those we would most like to know:
—how he was educated, particulars of his married life, his state
of health and, finally, the illness from which he died; knowledge
of all these would be invaluable for estimating his personal
relationship to his melancholy characters.

About his own character we know a great deal. I quote from
G. W. G. Wickham's Introduction to *The London Shakespeare*—
after reviewing the documentary evidence he continues as
follows:

"The picture of Shakespeare in London that results is of an
actor and poet who merged his twin talents into playwriting.
This brought him success enough to become a sharer in the
profits of two theatres, together with promotion into the
Sovereign's personal household. In an age which saw Marlowe
murdered, Ben Jonson in two fatal duels and other dramatists in
penury, no breath of scandal, social or political, attaches to his
name or blemishes the progressive success leading to retirement
at Stratford. The testimony of his contemporaries corroborates
this impression at every turn. If Ben Jonson alone rated him at

near his true stature, all his fellows speak of him as amiable and industrious, witty and of gentle disposition."

This then is the character presented to the world—the "persona". But we have also documentary evidence of the deeper personality, not so much from the plays, which are of necessity largely contrived, but from his poems—particularly the sonnets. These do not tell us Shakespeare's views on life or of the times in which he lived, but we do learn from them of a deep attachment to a fair boy and later to a dark lady. I will consider the nature of this attachment later.

What is most astonishing about Shakespeare is the genius of his characterizations, with excursions into psychological depths unplumbed by any dramatist before or since, anticipating the more scientific understanding of our own time. Francis Bacon, in his *Essays*, showed a similar fund of innate wisdom from which he drew his rules for the guidance of human conduct—but no such understanding of morbid psychology.

This remarkable faculty of Shakespeare's has induced people to believe that his plays could only have been written by a man of high rank and exceptional education. But the kind of genius he exhibits is intuitive and no more likely to be in the possession of a courtier than of an intelligent artisan.

I have been allowed to read and have permission to comment on an as yet unpublished work by a lady, Mrs D. Roberts, who believes in automatic writing. Her pen has been guided to produce dialogues of Socratic type, in which she interviews Shakespeare and various historical figures who claim to have had a hand in writing his plays, again through the medium of automatic writing—thus explaining the depth of his psychological perception. This idea of the collaboration of the best brains in history to produce Shakespeare's works is extended to identify various characters in the plays with each other, in accordance with the doctrine of "Karma"—the reincarnation of souls. Mrs Roberts reveals that *Hamlet* was inspired by the dead Sir Philip Sidney, related in turn to Antonio in *The Merchant of Venice* and to Prospero. Sir Thomas Meautys is the projected author of *Timon*. The only claim made by Bacon in these spiritualistic interviews is that he helped to edit the plays of Shakespeare.

The equation of the characters with their inspirers leads to some confusion between historical and fictional origins. Thus,

Jaques himself claims to have helped in the writing of *As You Like It*, whilst Gower and Thaisa assert their joint authorship of *Pericles*. Shakespeare himself is presented as the reincarnation of the young Lucius in *Julius Caesar*; he subsequently reappears as Lucius in *Cymbeline*—and historically as Edward II and Edward VI.

I may say that I do not accept this explanation for the enormous range of Shakespeare's experience, but I do not laugh at it, and I find it more interesting and even more plausible than the Baconian ciphers. One defect in this theory is that the historical characters concerned in the reincarnations are not sufficiently international—they include no figure from the Renaissance outside England. The soul of Leonardo da Vinci is possibly reserved for future men of science, but Michelangelo died just two months before the birth of Shakespeare, in whom his exceptional genius might surely have found a home.

Accepting that there was some faculty in Shakespeare's mind denied to other authors, I have considered whether his own psychological type might be a unique balance of all the possible characteristics, whereby he could view the world both as an introvert and extravert, with no bias towards any one of the four main functions. But I am satisfied that this is not so. The intuitive faculty is so strongly developed that I cannot deny it pre-eminence; I am also certain that most of his own self has gone into his introverted characters, of which a majority of my melancholics are examples.

It is not a defect in Shakespeare that the striking individuality of his characters is not matched by a corresponding originality in his plots. Aristotle makes no objection to adaptation from history and legend, whilst Freud finds as much significance in borrowed as in original material. He says that the writer selects those myths which fit in with his own unconscious desires, just as much as when his imagination is allowed free rein over the story.

The contrast in the moods of Shakespeare's tragedies and comedies is ascribed by Dr Somerville to his cyclo-thymic (or mildly manic-depressive) temperament, but I do not agree that an author's mind is reflected in his work in this particular way.

Although the characters here represented are mainly introverted, Shakespeare also delineated extraverted types with unerring precision. There is no extraverted thinking character in my survey, but I have quoted Jung's description of the main attributes of this type in my chapter on Antonio. The picture is that of a well-meaning, obstinate and often fanatical man, of which Angelo in *Measure for Measure* provides a ready example.

Extraverted, like introverted, feeling is a predominantly feminine characteristic. Jung's description is complicated, but the general impression is of a conventional woman who feels that the values accepted by her immediate circle must be right for her, without any reasoned explanation. Her feelings are capable of rapid change, just as a fashion may go into reverse; consequently she changes her mind frequently without feeling it necessary to account for this either to herself or to other people. The unconscious thinking function tends to be negative in character, producing vague and inexplicable fears, especially in relation to the objects most valued by her feelings.

Such women are not suitable figures for heroines or villainnesses, nor do they possess the attributes required for comedy. Constance, in *King John*, is the nearest example that comes to mind from Shakespeare's plays.

The next type, the sensation extravert, is most clearly represented by Falstaff, as I have mentioned in my chapter on Leontes, in which I have included a section of Jung's original description. To this I append an extension to cover Falstaff:

"Such a type—the majority are men apparently—does not, of course, believe himself to be 'subject' to sensation. He would be much more inclined to ridicule this view as altogether inconclusive, since, from his standpoint, sensation is the concrete manifestation of life—it is simply the fullness of actual living. His aim is concrete enjoyment and his morality is similarly orientated. For true enjoyment has its own special morality, its own moderation and lawfulness, its own unselfishness and devotedness. It by no means follows that he is just sensual or gross, for he may differentiate his sensation to the finest pitch of aesthetic purity without being the least unfaithful, even in his most abstract sensations, to his principle of objective sensation."

Extraverted intuition is seen most clearly in Macbeth and Lady Macbeth. Perhaps their tragedy is the possession of similar rather than complementary qualities, combined in the unrestraint of "vaulting ambition which o'erleaps itself". This opinion is supported by Ludwig Jekels, whom Freud quotes as regarding Macbeth and Lady Macbeth as psychologically one person.

I have given part of Jung's account of the extraverted intuitive personality in my chapter on Pericles. All this section is equally applicable to the Macbeths.

When one recalls Macbeth's: "to be thus is nothing, but to be safely thus", the following seems particularly apposite:

". . . a day will come when nothing will deter him from regarding as a prison the selfsame situation that seemed to promise him freedom and deliverance, and from acting accordingly."

A further paragraph is relevant to Macbeth's dependence on supernatural augury:

"The relative suppression of the functions of thinking and feeling leads to a claim to freedom and exemption from all restraint, since he suffers no submission of his decisions to rational judgement, relying entirely upon the perception of chance possibilities."

Of extraverted intuitive women Jung says:

". . . the intuitive activity reveals itself not so much in the professional as the social sphere. Such women understand the art of utilizing every social opportunity; they establish the right social connections; they seek out lovers with possibilities only to abandon everything for the sake of a new possibility."

Accepting that Shakespeare possessed an insight into, and a sympathy for, people of every psychological type, how are we to form a judgement of the occasions when particular characters express his own personal opinions and sentiments?

John Vyvyan says that Shakespeare nearly always allows his characters to express their own philosophy, but J. I. M. Stewart seems to contradict this by the following:

"A man writes plays partly at least because he is beset by unexpressed selves; by the subliminal falling now into one coherent pattern and now into another of the varied elements of that man."

Arthur Sewell quotes this view to disagree with it, but he admits that the tragic heroes seem to be conceived from within.

D. B. Wyndham Lewis has no doubt about it:

"In Shakespeare the spectators, the chorus, the doer and the god were all mixed up. He was all himself and certainly attached his own feelings to his characters."

I find two kinds of passage in which Shakespeare reveals himself particularly. In the first he puts into the mouths of his characters intellectual opinions which we may accept as his own, but which do not imply any identification of himself with the person who is speaking. Hamlet's advice to the Players, Polonius' lecture to Laertes and Jaques', "All the world's a stage" come into this category.

The second kind of passage is quite different. Scattered here and there in his plays there are isolated phrases or groups of lines of an emotional intensity in excess of or differing from the mood of the character in the particular context. It is impossible not to believe that in these places there is some besetting emotion which has forced itself into the writing, and that Shakespeare has momentarily identified himself with the speaker.

My first example is Orsino's:

> For women are as roses, whose fair flower
> Being once displayed doth fall that very hour,

followed by Viola's:

> And so they are: alas that they are so;
> To die, even when they to perfection grow.

Obviously Shakespeare cannot identify himself with Orsino and Viola at the same time; but there is an intensity in the lines suggestive of a special meaning in them for him. The sentiment, although originated by Ausonius, is not one which could be accepted from normal experience. It argues again that Shakespeare had no sexual interest in mature women—for one could hardly agree that feminine attractiveness is as evanescent as Orsino and Viola make it appear.

A cry which I have remarked in my chapter on *Hamlet* is his:

> Soft you now!
> The fair Ophelia! Nymph, in thy orisons
> Be all my sins remembered.

The intensity of this comes spontaneously and fades abruptly. The content of the preceding soliloquy, though deeply felt, is conceived intellectually; afterwards, Ophelia's cool rejection of Hamlet's gifts takes the heart out of him immediately.

A more prolonged *cri de cœur* comes from Prospero:

> The cloud-capped towers, the gorgeous palaces,
> The solemn temples, the great globe itself,
> Yea, all which it inherits, shall dissolve;
> And like this insubstantial pageant faded,
> Leave not a rack behind. We are such stuff
> As dreams are made on; and our little life
> Is rounded with a sleep.

He follows immediately with:

> Sir, I am vexed:
> Bear with my weakness. My old brain is troubled . . .

confirming the depth of emotion which has impelled Prospero's interruption of a merry carnival, and which one cannot doubt springs directly from the heart of the author.

But these examples are not confined to the introverted characters. Macbeth is allotted the emotionally charged passage beginning—"Tomorrow, and tomorrow, and tomorrow" during a scene of otherwise unreflective petulance. It is true that he has reason for unusual emotion from the shock of the Queen's sudden death, but the lines are so much out of character that Maurice Baring, in his amusing little play, *The Rehearsal*, attempted to explain them as an insertion of Shakespeare's at the instance of Burbadge, dissatisfied with the laconic but completely characteristic:

> She should have died hereafter:
> There would have been a time for such a word.

Surely the extra lines express Shakespeare's own feelings about the futility of much of the life around him.

To Theseus, a stiff and almost unactable character, is given the sudden inspiration:

> The poet's eye, in a fine frenzy rolling,
> Doth glance from heaven to earth, from earth to heaven;
> And as imagination bodies forth
> The forms of things unknown, the poet's pen
> Turns them to shapes, and gives to airy nothing
> A local habitation and a name.

This is the poet, Shakespeare, using as his mouthpiece a character plainly extraverted, but with no particularly predominant function in his colourless personality. Wilson Knight considers Theseus to be Shakespeare's own ideal of manhood, but I have never seen any actor make a success of the part.

Some of the passages which stand out from their context in this way are excessively short: I instance Antony's "Unarm, Eros, the long day's task is done." No doubt it will be objected that these lines are merely purple passages from Shakespeare's poetic inspiration rather than an expression of his own deep personal feeling; but to me they have a genuine and almost inexplicable nostalgic quality, of the kind known to the Roman poets as "desiderium".

These glimpses of Shakespeare's own thoughts and feelings show us what is apparent from the plays as a whole and from the opinions of his contemporaries: a poet wise and humane, with an all-pervading imagination and capable of the deepest feeling. He reveals himself through so many and diverse characters that particular identification can rarely be made.

A study of his non-dramatic works reveals a problem that has so worried his critics that the majority have taken refuge in rather feeble evasions. The fact is that Shakespeare wrote over a hundred sonnets addressed to a youth or "lovely boy", using terms as extravagant as those from any lover to his mistress or indeed as those in the smaller number of sonnets to the "dark lady". Dr Ernest Jones is convinced that in the latter Shakespeare's reproaches are directed to the lady more for her alienation of the boy's affections than for the withdrawal of her own.

The general argument of Shakespeare's defenders is that the extravagance of the language is merely poetic and respectful hyperbole such as was commonly used in addressing a noble patron at the time. Others are more ingenuous. Frank Harris says that if Shakespeare had been homosexually inclined it is impossible that homosexual feeling should not have manifested itself in his plays, amid such generous outpouring of human emotion. He also states that Shakespeare never wrote one ambiguous or tasteless line to embarrass his boy actors or the spectators watching them. My opinion is that, in a society which disapproves of homosexual relationships, it is unlikely that a playwright would introduce ideas certain to give general offence, whatever his personal inclinations—a study of Oscar Wilde's plays will confirm this. Also, it is only recently that a distinguished dramatic critic took exception to the playing of the "Induction" to *The Taming of the Shrew* exactly as Shakespeare wrote it, on the grounds that the dialogue between a man and a boy is indecent.

Ivor Brown has used attack as the best defence:

"It has been contended that Shakespeare's affection for the lovely boy outsteps propriety. That I think is no more than wishful thinking on the part of those who reject conventional morality."

The chain of reasoning can only be as follows: Shakespeare was good—therefore those who say that Shakespeare was homosexual must believe homosexuality to be good. I am afraid that the wishful thinking is demonstrably on the other side.

Surely Shakespeare settles the argument in Sonnet No. XX:

> A woman's face with nature's own hand painted
> Hast thou, the master-mistress of my passion;
> A woman's gentle heart, but not acquainted
> With shifting change, as is false woman's fashion;
> An eye more bright than theirs, less false in rolling,
> Gilding the object whereupon it gazeth;
> A man in hues, all hues in his controlling,
> Which steals men's eyes and women's souls amazeth.
> And for a woman wert thou first created,
> Till nature, as she wrought thee, fell a-doting,
> And by addition me of thee defeated
> By adding one thing to my purpose nothing.
> But since she pricked thee out for woman's pleasure,
> Mine be thy love and thy love's use their treasure.

It can hardly be seriously maintained that this is a poetic tribute of flattery to a distinguished patron, or that the sentiments are entirely platonic. But, having said this, I agree with Ivor Brown that the last four lines explicitly exclude any overt homosexual relationship.

It may be objected that, whilst the possession of homosexual feelings is not a matter for moral condemnation, the expression of them in writing is an affront to society and a betrayal in particular of the individual to whom the Sonnets are addressed. But there is no evidence that Shakespeare wrote the Sonnets for publication. His artistic fulfilment required him to express with his pen all that he felt most deeply, and it should be a matter for approbation that this part of his nature did not obtrude itself directly into his plays. It may be difficult for those in whom the word "homosexual" automatically arouses feelings of intense repugnance to appreciate that a great artist such as Shakespeare was great because of his capacity for experiencing every kind of human emotion, from which homosexual affection could not be excluded.

I have no wish to enter the competition for discovering the identity of the lovely boy or the dark lady. I do not even think it necessary for them to have had an independent existence; they may be, like the characters in the plays, creatures of Shakespear's own imagination—idealized types, or an epitome derived from a wide range of memory and experience.

Wyndham Lewis believes that Shakespeare's genius was feminine, so that he could create his female characters from a woman's point of view and fall in love with his own heroes.

Wilson Knight supports this idea:

"The essence of Shakespeare's art is the almost feminine abandon with which he sees into persons and forces generally."

It would be wrong to adduce from these opinions a passive form of homosexual temperament in Shakespeare, or to link them with his affection for the lovely boy—a relationship implying no femininity in the older partner. As I have noted in my chapter on Antonio, homosexuality is not a single specific entity, but embraces a variety of attitudes with many degrees, only some of which can be considered genuinely perverse.

So far as the plays are concerned, I accept that Shakespeare had a subjective understanding of sexuality in all its manifestations, without which his characters would have been infinitely less human and his melancholics less individual and less subtly delineated.

To relate Shakespeare's day to day or year to year experiences to his plays is a different and even more speculative venture. I think it totally wrong to visualize in the poet the mood of the play which he is writing at the time. Great art is not produced under conditions of profound mental stress; in particular, a state of depression—or melancholia—reduces the capacity for experiencing and transmitting emotional impulses of all kinds, whether pleasant or unpleasant. Tchaikowsky's "profound despair", alleged to be responsible for his *Pathetic Symphony*, was a neurotic rather than truly depressive condition, and Schumann produced no musical works in the asylum where he spent his later years.

Shakespeare's inspiration was intellectual and spiritual rather than emotional, and the sequence of his plays reflects his growing absorption, first in the mixture of tragedy and comedy which he found in life, and later in the possibility of a hidden meaning behind it. It is natural that the earlier plays should show little concern for a solution to the problem dramatized, whereas the more contemplative Shakespeare should in his maturity become more and more engrossed with the metaphysical aspects of human behaviour. Finally he leaves all questions answered—by purgation of the soul from guilt preparatory to the happy ending which all Christian men of his time devoutly aspired to. In this context the events in the life of the poet himself and in the world about him rank as of small consequence compared to the wider vision revealed from his inner perception.

Although I reject a specific influence of outside events upon the mood of Shakespeare's plays, it is natural that he should identify himself more with some characters than with others. In their search for the particular microcosms of Shakespeare's self most critics seem to have overlooked the obvious factor of age. Not only are characters nearest in age to Shakespeare himself at the time he was writing most likely to express his own emotional and intellectual strivings, but it is also likely that his views at the age of fifty will differ markedly from those he held in his twenties.

Ivor Brown, borrowing from "The seven ages of man", divides the plays into seven groups, which I accept as convenient landmarks, without entering into disputation about the exact chronology. T. W. Baldwin hazards a much earlier date for several, on the assumption that the company produced two plays a year and that the more commonly accepted dates were those of repeat productions. *The London Shakespeare*, in striking averages between the extremes of projected dates, neglects the years prior to 1591 and crowds an almost impossible number of plays into the period 1593–96. The differences between these three authorities are noted in an appendix.

About the last group there is a general consensus of agreement: the period is that between 1609 and 1612, and the accepted order—*Cymbeline, The Winter's Tale, The Tempest* and *Henry VIII*. I have noted reasons for placing *Timon* before *Lear* and *Twelfth Night* before *As You Like It*, but do not wish to express any views of my own apart from this.

The first group of plays given by Ivor Brown includes the three parts of *Henry VI, Titus Andronicus, The Comedy of Errors, The Taming of the Shrew, Richard III* and *The Two Gentlemen of*

*Verona*. These he classes as 'prentice efforts, and I do not think we need search for the heart of Shakespeare in any. In the early historical plays his one outstanding characterization is Richard III, the foundation for which was laid by Sir Thomas More. Freud concedes a point to Adler by ascribing the villainy of Shakespeare's Richard III to an exaction of reparation from the world for his deformity.

*Titus Andronicus* is an exercise in Senecan tragedy, and *The Two Gentlemen of Verona* is remarkable for the characters only of Launce and his dog. *The Comedy of Errors* and *The Taming of the Shrew* are Shakespeare's sole essays into farce apart from *The Merry Wives of Windsor*. The former has never been highly esteemed, although Komisarjevsky's 1938 production was an outstanding success. The *Shrew*, though dramatically more effective, I do not believe to contain Shakespeare's mature views on the relationship between husbands and wives.

Ivor Brown's next group—the Lyrical—comprises the poems *Venus and Adonis*, *Lucrece* and the early Sonnets, with the plays *Love's Labour's Lost*, *Romeo and Juliet*, *A Midsummer Night's Dream* and *The Merchant of Venice*—written during the period 1592–96. Critics, including Robert Speaight and Ivor Brown himself, commonly identify Shakespeare with Berowne, but none with Romeo. I agree that Berowne may well represent Shakespeare in his late twenties. The wit and verbal felicity of the character accord well with what we know of him, and the by-play of love between Berowne and Rosaline may be a product of his own experience. The name Rosaline seems to have a significance for Shakespeare, but I do not go so far as Ivor Brown and Frank Harris, who identify her with the dark lady of the Sonnets.

Romeo is much younger than his creator, and despite the poetic beauty of his lines I have never felt satisfied of the depth or eternity of his love for Juliet. His inconstancy shows itself in his quick abandonment of the other Rosaline; and to me the tragedy of the play is that, but for the opposition of their families and the error with the potion, they would have drifted out of love as easily as they drifted in, leaving them with an experience of evanescent charm to be recollected only with faint nostalgia in their maturity.

In *A Midsummer Night's Dream* the main theme is the love entanglements of four couples, explored at no great depth—the whole subordinated to the contrast between the fantastic wiles of the immortals and the earthy stolidity of the artisans. Theseus is perhaps the character nearest to Shakespeare in age, but apart from expressing some laudable views on the toleration of amateur dramatics and the one significant speech about love, lunacy and poetry, he is an unsubstantial figure presiding uneasily over the affairs of lovers and rustics alike.

The first melancholy character appears at the end of this period—in *The Merchant of Venice*, written in 1595–96. Antonio is of similar age to Shakespeare at the time, and his relationship to Bassanio has some affinity with that of Shakespeare and the "lovely boy" of the Sonnets—with the distinction that I believe Shakespeare to have been wholly aware of the nature of the attraction which he experienced, whereas I have given grounds for presuming that Antonio's feelings are repressed. The inclusion of the early Sonnets amongst Shakespeare's compositions in this period fortifies me in my opinion that Shakespeare did not proceed further with the character of Antonio because he unconsciously shrank from its full implications.

Leslie Hotson has a different view about the Sonnets, dating the early group around 1588–89, on the basis of what he regards as references to the Spanish Armada and to the eclipses of the period. He relates the Sonnets to outside events rather than to those in Shakespeare's life. Nevertheless, he embarks on his own search for the identity of the fair boy, ranging so discursively that one is left uncertain of his final choice.

From 1596–99 Shakespeare was occupied with the historical plays: *King John, Richard II, Henry IV*, 1 and 2 and *Henry V*. I agree with Ivor Brown and others that a personal note must have crept into the treatment of Arthur in *King John*, following the death of Shakespeare's eleven-year-old son, Hamnet—in 1596. In the moving scene in the Tower he can hardly have failed to identify himself with Hubert, giving to that comparatively minor figure an expression of emotion deeper than is found in the lines of more important characters. Mrs Roberts's pen is guided to note the spirit of Hamnet as the inspiration also of William's lesson in *The Merry Wives of Windsor*.

In *Richard II* Shakespeare's balancing of contrasted characters surpasses anything that he has done before. The introvert and contemplative Richard is set against the extravert and active Bolingbroke, whose humanity is in turn countered by the fanaticism of Northumberland. Then there are the two elder Dukes—Gaunt, the one man strong enough to hold the kingdom together, were he not too old and too sick—York, the retiring country gentleman, instinctively loyal to the Crown but quite out of his element in battle and in high affairs of state. All these characters are acutely observed, but essentially from without; had there been any man about with Shakespeare's instinct for statesmanship the tragedy would never have happened.

In *Henry IV* Shakespeare's great creation is Sir John Falstaff, but though we may laugh with him and enjoy his misdemeanours his weaknesses are not those of the dramatist but of a contrary type for which he has a profound affection and a forgiving sympathy.

The next group of plays, described by Ivor Brown as "High Fantastical", comprises four comedies—written between 1599 and 1601; *The Merry Wives of Windsor, Much Ado about Nothing, Twelfth Night* and *As You Like It*.

*The Merry Wives of Windsor*, his final essay into farce, shows traces of hasty composition and may well have been commissioned by the Queen, anxious to see Falstaff in love, as has been suggested. Of more interest than the Knight in the declension of his former wit is the character of Ford, the first of Shakespeare's jealous husbands. I have given reasons for preferring Orsino as the precursor of the truly jealous type, but Claudio in *Much Ado* also lends a ready ear to the imputation of unfaithfulness in his betrothed.

It has been asserted by Dover Wilson and agreed by others that from 1601 onwards a "strain of sex nausea" runs through Shakespeare's plays; some experience of his own at about this time is adduced to account for this. It seems to me more likely that he was a portrayer of human nature too sincere to romanticize sexual love for the purpose of the stage as has been done by other dramatists from time immemorial, and that his observations on the relationship between the sexes are those of a realist—not disillusioned, but without illusions. *The Merchant of Venice* and *As You Like It* are really his only plays in which the course of true love runs comparatively smooth, and in all the plays there are pitfalls and reservations. In the group under consideration the sexual appetite of the senescent is exposed to crude mockery, whilst Claudio, Orsino and Sebastian are hardly exhibited as ideal mates. From his own experience and that of the world Shakespeare was well aware of the infrequency of ennobling activity in the sexual instinct and the far more common perversity and contradiction with the rest of the character which make it such a fascinating—and at times almost horrifying—study.

We know that Shakespeare married a wife six years older than himself, certainly pregnant at the time, and that he had a vision of a provocative dark lady. But I do not think that any particular sequence of personal sexual experience can be inferred from the ordering of his plays.

The views on ideal marriage given through the mouth of Orsino I believe to be those of Shakespeare, without otherwise identifying him with that character. I am convinced that Jaques, in this group, is the nearest approach to Shakespeare himself that has yet appeared. In 1601, at 37, he was well into middle life according to the conceptions of his time, and ready to abandon the activities of young manhood for a more contemplative existence.

I cannot accept Ivor Brown's separate group of "Bitter Comedies", from 1601–3. The three plays concerned: *All's Well that Ends Well*, *Troilus and Cressida* and *Measure for Measure* overlap with the tragedies in any system. *All's Well* seems immature work—Baldwin postulates a much earlier production, in 1589 in conjunction with *The Comedy of Errors*. *Troilus and Cressida* is a roistering bawdy play, part comedy, part tragedy, stripping the ancient Greeks of their godlike panoply and reducing them to mortal stature. This seems to have been a misconception of Shakespeare's, because it is just that close relationship with the gods that makes the Greek heroes dramatically interesting; in their reduced status they become petty whilst remaining remote, and I class Shakespeare's experiment as a failure.

*Measure for Measure* presents a new aspect of life: the bigotry that, uncontrolled, leads to tyranny and eventually to war. In this case the controlling force, the Duke, has abrogated his authority. Perhaps Shakespeare, in his identification with Jaques abjuring the world, has become aware of the danger to government when men of sense and humanity become so disgusted with authority that they decide to shrug their shoulders and leave what we now call "the cosmic mess" to someone else. To this extent can Shakespeare be identified with the truant Duke.

The moral issue of chastity against life is another of Shakespeare's conundrums to which he gives no certain answer; but I do not find in this an essentially bitter approach.

The years 1601–8, entitled by Ivor Brown "The Dark Vision", contain most of the tragedies. The complete list is: *Julius Caesar, Hamlet, Othello, Macbeth, Timon of Athens, King Lear, Coriolanus* and *Antony and Cleopatra*. Ivor Brown includes the "dark lady" sonnets in this period.

Shakespeare is now concerned with more serious issues, but this is a natural result of his maturity and the more certain aim of his poetic vision. It is not necessary to postulate tragic circumstances in his own life or in the world around him.

The main feature of *Julius Caesar* is, as in *Richard II*, the contrast of characters: the extravert thinking Cassius and the introvert intuitive Brutus, who is again contrasted with the extravert intuitive Antony. Of these characters, Shakespeare's own sympathies seem to be most with Brutus. The succession of the same psychological type, in Hamlet, suggests to me that this was the basic type of Shakespeare himself. All great art requires high development of the intuitive faculty, and introversion is suggested by the profound understanding of men of all types which is Shakespeare's pre-eminent quality.

In *Othello* and *Macbeth* Shakespeare returns to the study of the extraverted type. Othello's fixation on the sexual purity of Desdemona, culminating in his fanatical cry: "It is the cause, it is the cause, my soul!" is the epitome of the thinking extravert. Macbeth's extraverted intuition is exemplified by his dependence upon omens and his "nose" for opportunities of self-advancement. Shakespeare seems to be outside both these characters, arousing our feelings of pity without the conviction that in other circumstances they could have ordered their affairs aright. Wilson Knight finds *Macbeth* essentially different from the other great tragedies, equating his theme with that of Angelo—perhaps because of the extraversion of the characters.

I have given reasons for placing *Timon* before *Lear* and for classifying both titular subjects as sensation introverts. In these characters, even more than in Hamlet, something seems to come out from the very core of Shakespeare's personality, but in a distorted form. As an intuitive type, Shakespeare would have strongly repressed leanings towards sensation which might well emerge in this bizarre dramatic imagery.

Coriolanus is another introvert, who is particularly lacking in intuition. He has no idea of the impact of his own personality upon the Romans, and I classify him also as a predominantly sensation type.

The Antony of *Antony and Cleopatra* is not the Antony of *Julius Caesar*. His intuitive orientation has given way to sensation. He lives for the appetite of the day, with little foreboding of the future; but the basic type is still extraverted. Ivor Brown has a theory that the emergence of this apotheosis of mature love was due to Shakespeare's release from the bonds of the faithless dark lady, whom he presumes to have died. Frank Harris invokes a correspondence between most of Shakespeare's female characters and the women in his own life, including his mother, his wife, his daughters and the dark lady. Ivor Brown follows him in idealizing Cleopatra as the woman the dark lady might have been, shorn of her mortal imperfections; but the tendency of recent criticism is to deprecate these unsubstantiated identifications.

I do not see "Sweet Mr Shakespeare" in the role of military conqueror and great lover, and I find more of him on the sidelines with Enobarbus, the introverted character to whom much of the descriptive poetry is given.

The final plays, written between 1608 and 1613, are neatly defined by Ivor Brown as "Fancy-free". In these plays the art of Shakespeare takes an individual line derived from no predecessor and which succeeding playwrights have made no attempt to follow. I pass over *Henry VIII*, a large part of which is presumed to have been written by Fletcher, and which is in any case more a masque than a play, written, like the *Merry Wives*, to order rather than by the urgency of Shakespeare's own dramatic inspiration. The remaining plays are *Pericles*, *Cymbeline*, *The Winter's Tale* and *The Tempest*.

These final plays, more mature, more complex and more highly individual than their predecessors, are nevertheless not so dramatically effective. The rapid succession of scenes in *Pericles* is bewildering and the final act of *Cymbeline* implausible. Even in *The Tempest* the action does not carry the play along. The long-drawn-out account of Prospero's early history plainly bores Miranda and can hardly fail to bore the audience; the scene of the Court's arrival on the island is only relieved from tedium after the older gentlemen have been mercifully charmed to sleep. These plays are, notwithstanding, Shakespeare's supreme achievement, yielding more and more of their hidden charm through the experience of repeated performance.

The authorship of *Pericles* is again in dispute, but the theme of father-daughter relationship and the miraculous resuscitations place it fairly in Shakespeare's last period. Pericles, like Macbeth, is an extraverted type, but whereas Macbeth operates almost wholly on a conscious level, the repressed material of the incest theme smothers the intuition of Pericles—as if Shakespeare had turned himself inside-out: to that extent is Pericles part of him.

In all four plays, as might be expected from Shakespeare at his time of life, the women are more important as daughters than as wives, but the fathers are not necessarily embodiments of Shakespeare. Cymbeline is a weak character, not even a Theseus or a Duke Senior, bearing a resemblance to the hardly "grand old" Duke of York in *Richard II*. He fails in what should be his function of holding the play together, and in the end his role seems to be taken over by Bellarius. It would be interesting to study these two characters as opposing elements in Shakespeare himself, but this would require a separate chapter.

In *The Winter's Tale* the characterization is weaker than usual. The brilliant study of paranoia in Leontes is allowed to fade out, leaving Perdita as the only figure of real dramatic interest in the later part of the play. Unusually for Shakespeare *The Winter's Tale* is a play of ideas rather than character, with a particular idea predominating: the novelty, in the dramatic world, of the power of repentance and forgiveness. Neither in Leontes nor in any other character is the personal Shakespeare apparent; he emerges, like Ariel from the cloven pine, after twelve years in the hermit's cell which he entered as Jaques.

Wilson Knight reminds us of the similar hermit-like isolation of Timon and Bellarius. Both he and L. C. Knights attach much importance to the element of time in Shakespeare. Prospero has been on his island for twelve years, corresponding to the period covered by Shakespeare's greatest plays. For twelve years previously Ariel had been imprisoned in the pine, a circumstance which Wilson Knight equates with Shakespeare's early dramatic period.

In no other play of Shakespeare's, not even in *Hamlet*, is a character so dominant as Prospero in *The Tempest*. It is true that Ariel and Caliban are never far in the background, but most critics recognize them as psychologically and dramatically a part of Prospero himself.

Prospero is of the same psychological type as Jaques—the thinking introvert. I have said that I consider intuition the dominant function in Shakespeare, as in Hamlet, but an integration of these two qualities makes for a soundly balanced character. Whatever Hamlet's views may be on "the pale cast of thought", a more reasoned and less intuitive approach to his problem could have solved it without tragedy, whilst Jaques is aware that could he but catch some of the intuition of Touchstone his cynicism would be mellowed to the benefit of all.

Prospero, like Hamlet, with whom Wilson Knight also notes an affinity, has been deposed by the action of a relative, but his banishment gives him time for contemplation. Older and less impulsive than Hamlet, the tolerance of his added years makes him receptive to the counsel of Ariel—his better self. His attitude to Gonzalo is particularly revealing; it is as if Hamlet were apologizing to the shade of Polonius for his treatment of one regarded by others as "the good old man". Wilson Knight finds in Gonzalo a blend of Polonius, Adam and Kent. It is interesting to note that T. W. Baldwin allots the roles of Polonius, Kent and Gonzalo all to John Heminges; there is contemporary evidence that Shakespeare himself played Adam.

In Freudian terms, the psyche of Prospero embraces Caliban —the id—and Ariel—the ego-ideal. The more complex structure of Jung can find room for most of the components of the play. Caliban is the dark shadow in the depths of the psyche; Antonio and Sebastian reinforce him at a more subliminal level. Miranda is the anima—the ideal of womanhood, and Gonzalo the archetypal wise old man. Colin Still finds analogies in folklore and in the Christian religion. He quotes a sixteenth-century Chinese story of a hero-saint—Tripitaka—who is accompanied on a pilgrimage by two servants, Monkey and Pigsey, plainly analogous to Ariel and Caliban. In his Christian embodiment, Prospero is God, Ariel the Angel of the Lord and Caliban the Devil.

Robert Speaight, remarking that Hamlet is the only one of Shakespeare's characters who could have written his plays, adds that after *Hamlet* it is left to Prospero to restore to man both his reason and his *raison d'être*. He does this by the abandonment of his protective "persona"—that of the wizard, the maker of spells. Now that his defence against the world is lowered to admit of forgiveness for his enemies he can stand on his own, a re-integrated personality, in the words of John Vyvyan: "ethically sufficiently evolved to substitute mercy for justice". Similarly, Shakespeare the dramatist has fulfilled his task; he can spend his remaining years as Shakespeare the man.

I have made little reference to the women in Shakespeare's plays, as I have been concerned with his revelation of himself in particular through his melancholy characters. Ivor Brown would have it that he truly loved his heroines, and H. B. Charlton regards the women in his comedies as more sensitive to intuition and more responsive to emotion than the men. But I must admit that I find them less satisfactory than his heroes. I do not think this is because the parts were written for performance by boys—the subtlety of Cleopatra negatives this idea. Of them all I am most affected by Viola and least by Rosalind, an impression confirmed by memorable performances of each part by the same leading actress. I believe that the reason for this is Shakespeare's greater sympathy for Orsino than for Orlando. Nothing that he wrote about love, even in *Antony and Cleopatra*, quite attains the depth of feeling between Viola and the as yet unawakened Orsino.

To summarize the characters which I have chosen to represent the melancholics: I find much of the unconscious Shakespeare in Antonio; none in Don John; Shakespeare the lover in Orsino; the thinker in Jaques; the intuitive in Hamlet, and Shakespeare inside-out in Pericles. Timon I regard as an example of a mind diseased and Leontes an interesting puppet in a play of ideas. I reserve for Prospero the embodiment of the fully mature and integrated Shakespeare. This integration is illustrated by the introjective relation of the other characters to Prospero and enhanced by the observation, noted by Paul Stapfer, for the first and last time in Shakespeare's plays, of all the unities demanded by Aristotle.

# CHRONOLOGICAL TABLE

| IVOR BROWN | T. W. BALDWIN | LONDON SHAKESPEARE |
|---|---|---|
| *Henry VI*, 1, 2, and 3 | | |
| *Titus Andronicus* | *Love's Labour's Lost* | |
| *The Comedy of Errors* | *All's Well that Ends Well* | |
| | *The Comedy of Errors* | |
| *The Taming of the Shrew* | *Two Gentlemen of Verona* | |
| | *Henry V* | |
| *Richard III* | *Romeo and Juliet* | *Henry VI*, 1 |
| | *Henry VI*, 1, 2, and 3 | |
| *The Two Gentlemen of Verona* | *Titus Andronicus* | *Henry VI*, 2 and 3 |
| *Venus and Adonis* | *The Merry Wives of Windsor* | *The Comedy of Errors; Venus and Adonis* |
| *Love's Labour's Lost* | *Hamlet* | *Richard III; Thomas More* |
| *The Rape of Lucrece* | *Richard III* | *Titus Andronicus* |
| *Romeo and Juliet* | *A Midsummer Night's Dream* | *The Taming of the Shrew* |
| | *The Taming of the Shrew* | *The Rape of Lucrece* |
| *A Midsummer Night's Dream* | *King John* | *Love's Labour's Lost* |
| | *Richard II* | *Romeo and Juliet; Two Gentlemen of Verona* |
| *Early Sonnets* | *Henry IV*, 1 | *A Midsummer Night's Dream; Richard II* |
| *King John* | *Henry IV*, 2 | *The Merchant of Venice; King John* |
| *Richard II* | *The Merchant of Venice* | *The Merry Wives of Windsor* |
| *? The Merchant of Venice* | *Love's Labour's Lost* (repeat) | *Henry IV*, 1 and 2 |
| *Henry IV*, 1 and 2 | *Romeo and Juliet* (repeat) | *Much Ado about Nothing* |
| | *Much Ado about Nothing* | *Henry V* |
| *Henry V* | *Henry V* | *Julius Caesar; Sonnets* |
| *The Merry Wives of Windsor* | *Julius Caesar* | *As You Like It* |
| | *As You Like It* | *Twelfth Night* |
| *Much Ado about Nothing* | *Twelfth Night* | |
| *? Julius Ceasar* | *Troilus and Cressida* | |
| *Twelfth Night* | | *Hamlet* |
| *As You Like It* | | *All's Well that Ends Well* |
| *Hamlet*; Later Sonnets | | *Troilus and Cressida* |
| *All's Well that Ends Well* | *Hamlet* (repeat) | |
| *Troilus and Cressida* | *The Merry Wives of Windsor* (repeat) | *Othello* |
| *Measure for Measure* | | |
| | *Othello* | *Measure for Measure* |
| *Othello* | *Measure for Measure* | |
| | *Timon of Athens* | *King Lear* |
| *Macbeth* | *King Lear* | |
| *King Lear* | *Macbeth* | *Macbeth* |
| *Timon of Athens* | *Antony and Cleopatra* | *Antony and Cleopatra* |
| | *All's Well that Ends Well* (repeat) | *Timon of Athens* |
| *Coriolanus* | *Pericles* | *Pericles* |
| | *Coriolanus* | *Coriolanus* |
| *Antony and Cleopatra* | | |
| *Pericles* | | *Cymbeline* |
| | *Cymbeline* | *The Winter's Tale* |
| *Cymbeline* | *The Winter's Tale* | *The Tempest* |
| *The Winter's Tale* | *The Tempest* | |
| *The Tempest* | *Henry VIII* | *Henry VIII* |
| *Henry VIII* | | |

# BIBLIOGRAPHY

ADLER, Alfred. *International Journal of Individual Psychology.* London, C. W. Daniel. Various dates, 1932–38

ARISTOTLE. *Poetics.* Trans.: W. Hamilton Fyfe. London, Heinemann, 1927.

BABB, Lawrence. *The Elizabethan Malady, A Study of Melancholia in English Literature from 1580 to 1640.* Michigan State College Press, East Lansing, 1951.

BALDWIN, T. W. *The Organization and Personnel of the Shakespearean Company.* Princeton University Press, 1927.

BARKER, Harley Granville. *Prefaces to Shakespeare.* London, Batsford, 1930.

BETHELL, S. L. *The Winter's Tale, a Study.* London, Staples Press, 1948.

BRIGHT, Timothy. *Treatise of Melancholy, 1586.*

BROOKE, Stopford A. *Ten Plays of Shakespeare.* London, Constable, 1905.

IBID. *Ten More Plays of Shakespeare.* London, Constable, 1913.

BROWN, Ivor. *Shakespeare.* London, Collins, 1949.

BURTON, Robert. *The Anatomy of Melancholy (1621).* Tudor Publishing Co., 1938.

CHARLTON, H. B. *Shakespearean Comedy.* London, Methuen, 1938.

COLERIDGE, S. T. *Shakespeare Notes and Lectures.* Ed.: Edward Howell. Liverpool, 1875.

DRYDEN, John. *Dramatic Poesy and Other Lectures* (Everyman Library). London, Dent, 1939.

ELIOT, T. S. *The Sacred Wood.* London, Methuen, 1948.

EYSENCK, H. J. *Abnormal Psychology.* London, Pitman, 1960.

FREUD, Sigmund. *Collected Papers,* Vol. IV. London, Hogarth Press, 1953.

GARDNER, Helen. *As You Like It* (from *More Talking of Shakespeare.* Ed.: John Garrett). London, Hodder & Stoughton, 1959.

GOLLANCZ, Sir Israel. *The Sources of Hamlet.* Oxford University Press, 1926.

HARRIS, Frank. *The Women of Shakespeare.* London, Methuen, 1911.

HARRISON, G. B. *Introducing Shakespeare*. London, Pelican Books, 1939.

HOTSON, Leslie. *The First Night of "Twelfth Night"*. London, Rupert Hart-Davies, 1954.

IBID. *Shakespeare's Sonnets Dated*. London, Rupert Hart-Davies, 1949.

HUDSON, Rev. H. N. *Shakespeare, His Life, Art and Character*. 2 Vols. Boston, Ginn, 1872.

INGLEBY, C. M. *Shakespeare Hermeneutics, or The Still Lion*. London, Trübner, 1875.

JACOBI, Iolande. *The Psychology of C. G. Jung*. London, Routledge & Kegan Paul, 1942.

JOHNSON, Samuel. *Johnson on Shakespeare*. Ed.: Walter Raleigh. Oxford University Press, 1940.

JONES, Ernest. *Hamlet and Oedipus*. London, Gollancz, 1949.

JONSON, Ben. *Ben Jonson*. Ed.: C. H. Herford and Percy Simpson. Oxford, 1925–.

JOSEPH, Bertram. *Conscience and The King, a Study of Hamlet*. London, Chatto & Windus, 1953.

JUNG, Carl Gustav. *Psychological Types*. Trans.: H. Godwin Baynes. London, Kegan Paul, 1933.

IBID. *Modern Man in Search of a Soul*. London, Kegan Paul, 1933.

KNIGHT, G. Wilson. *The Crown of Life*. London, Methuen, 1948.

IBID. *The Wheel of Fire*. Oxford University Press, 1930.

IBID. *The Sovereign Flower*. London, Methuen, 1958.

IBID. *The Shakespearean Tempest*. Oxford University Press, 1932.

KNIGHTS, L. C. *Some Shakespearean Themes*. London, Chatto & Windus, 1959.

LEVIN, Harry. *The Question of Hamlet*. Oxford University Press, 1957.

LEWIS, D. B. Wyndham. *The Lion and the Fox*. London, Methuen, 1951.

MCDOUGALL, William. *Outline of Psychology*. London, Methuen, 1923.

MAXWELL, J. C. *Timon of Athens (The New Shakespeare)*. Cambridge University Press, 1957.

MUIR, Kenneth. *Shakespeare's Sources*. London, Methuen, 1957.

MURRAY, Gilbert. *Hamlet and Orestes*. British Academy Annual Shakespeare Lecture. London, Milford, 1914.

OLIVER, H. J. *Timon of Athens (Arden Shakespeare)*. London, Methuen, 1959.

PLUTARCH. *Life of Alcibiades*. Trans.: J. W. Langhorne. London, Walter Scott Publishing Co., N.D.

IBID. *Life of Antony*. Trans.: John Dryden, revised A. Clough. London, Dent, 1910.

POPE, Alexander. *The Works of Shakespeare*, in 6 Vols. London, Jacob Tonson, 1725.

ROBERTS, Mrs Daisy, and Allen E. Woolcock, M.Sc. *Shakespearean Episode*. Personal Communication.

SEWELL, Arthur. *Character and Society in Shakespeare*. Oxford, Clarendon Press, 1951.

SOMERVILLE, H. *Madness in Shakespearean Tragedy*. London, Richards Press, 1929.

SPEAIGHT, Robert. *Nature in Shakespearean Tragedy*. London, Hollis & Carter, 1955.

STAPFER, Paul. *Shakespeare and Classical Antiquity*. Trans.: Emily J. Carey. London, Kegan Paul, 1880.

STEWART, J. I. M. *Character and Motive in Shakespeare*. London, Longman's Green, 1949.

STILL, Colin. *The Timeless Theme*. London, Nicholson & Watson, 1936.

STRONG, L. A. G. *Shakespeare and Psychology* (from *Talking of Shakespeare*. Ed.: John Garrett). London, Hodder & Stoughton, 1954.

THOMSON, Sir St Clair. "Shakespeare and Medicine." Reprinted from *Transactions of the Medical Society of London*. London, Harrison & Sons, 1916.

TILLYARD, E. M. W. *Shakespeare's Last Plays*. London, Chatto & Windus, 1951.

ULRICI, Hermann. *Shakespeare's Dramatic Art* (trans.). London, Chapman Bros., 1846.

VYVYAN, John. *The Shakespearean Ethic*. London, Chatto & Windus, 1959.

WATSON, George. *Three Ways to Shakespeare*. Broadcast Lecture, B.B.C. Third Programme, August 1960.

WEBSTER, Margaret. *Shakespeare Today*. London, J. M. Dent, 1957

WICKHAM, G. W. G. *Introduction to the London Shakespeare*. London, Eyre & Spottiswoode, 1958.

WILSON, John Dover. *What Happens in Hamlet*. Cambridge University Press, 1935.

# GENERAL INDEX

*New London Shakespeare, The* 147
North, Sir Thomas 122

*Ode on the Intimations of Immortality* 161
Oedipus 101, 102, 105
Oliver, H. J. 113
Orestes 92, 100, 102
Orsino, Virginio 56
d'Osset, Cardinal 56
*Othello* 16, 178, 183
Ovid 57

*Pandosto* 156
Pathetic Symphony, The 172
*Pattern of Painful Adventures* 131
*il Penseroso* 23
*Pericles, Prince of Tyre* 131–144, 152, 155, 165, 179, 180, 183
Phillips, Augustine 60
Plutarch 117, 122
Pope, Alexander 11, 15
Potter, Stephen 31
Pound, Ezra 37
*Psychological Types* 13, 45
*Purification, The* 144

Quixote, Don 102

*Rehearsal, The* 169
*Richard II* 175, 178, 179, 183
*Richard III* 173, 183
Roberts, Mrs Daisy 164, 175
*Rocke of Regarde, The* 48
*Romeo and Juliet* 174

Saxo Grammaticus 99
*Schoole of Abuse, The* 41
Schumann, R. A. 172
Sewell, Arthur 14, 16, 35, 68, 76, 124, 158, 159, 167
*Shakespeare Allusion Book, The* 163
Shakespeare, Anne, *see* Hathaway
Shakespeare, Edmund 108, 126
Shakespeare, Hamnet 175
Shakespeare, John 106
Shakespeare, William, *passim*
Shaw, G. B. 69

Sidney, Sir Philip 164
*Sinister Street* 146
*Skin of Our Teeth, The* 141
Socrates 117
Somerville, H. 77, 124, 125, 165
*Sonnets, The* 46, 58, 164, 170–172, 174, 175, 178, 183
Speaight, Robert 76, 89, 97, 98, 102, 174, 181
Stapfer, P. 122, 182
Stewart, J. I. M. 13, 42, 63, 156, 157, 158, 167
Still, C. 181
Stratford, theatre at 139
Strong, L. A. G. 17, 42, 56, 101, 126
*Suddenly Last Summer* 58

*Taming of the Shrew, The* 170, 173, 174, 183
Tavistock Clinic, the 29
Tchaikovsky, P. 172
*Tempest, The* 72, 145, 173, 179, 180, 183
Thomson, Sir St C. 114
Tillyard, E. M. W. 156, 161
*Timon of Athens* 16, 108–130, 164, 173, 178, 183
*Timon the Misanthrope* 122, 123
*Titus Andronicus* 48, 173, 174, 183
Tolstoy, Leo 126
Tripitaka 181
*Troilus and Cressida* 177, 183
*Twelfth Night* 50–60, 72, 173, 176, 183
Twine, L. 131
*Two Gentlemen of Verona, The* 44, 173, 174, 183
*Turn of the Screw, The* 14

Ulrici, H. 64, 144
'*Ur-Hamlet*' 99

*Venus and Adonis* 174, 183
*Ville dont le Prince est un Enfant, La* 43
da Vinci, Leonardo 165
Vyvyan, J. 13, 106, 128, 129, 143, 145, 158, 159, 167, 182

# INDEX OF CHARACTERS